Writers Around The Mulberry Tree

An Anthology

Edward Gaskell
DEVON

Edward Gaskell publishers
Riverbank Cottages
Bideford
Devon
EX39 2QR

First published 2018

ISBN 978-1-906769-79-6

© All Contributors

Writers Around the Mulberry Tree

An Anthology

All rights reserved. No part of this publication may be reproduced, stored in a retrieval system, or transmitted in any form by any means electronic, mechanical, photocopying, scanning, recording or otherwise, without the prior written permission of the publishers.

Typeset, printed and bound by
Lazarus Press
6 Grenville Street
Bideford
Devon
EX39 3DX
www.lazaruspress.com

CONTENTS

1	Introduction	5
2	Susie Lyons	7
3	Angela Nurse	11
4	Ann Thomas	38
5	Anne Smith	60
6	Barbara Ferris	87
7	Barbara Johnson	113
8	Diana Warmington	142
9	Elizabeth Fowler	169
10	Eric Smith	193
11	Richard Small	223
12	Sally Ferdinando	254
13	Joint Stories	261

Edward Gaskell
Publishers
DEVON

The Mulberry Tree Writers

The Mulberry Tree Writers meet weekly almost all year round in the All Saints Community Chapel, Instow.

Considering how frequently we meet together, the output of gifted writing is extraordinary.

Very sadly, since the first draft of our anthology going to press, our dear friend Eric Smith has died. We have many of his stories and poems in this book and in his second book of poems, 'Poems for Pleasure', which was published for him to see and enjoy in June of this year (2017).

We dedicate this anthology to him and I include the following short story inspired by him. Not difficult, he inspired us all.

Susan Lyons

Eric Smith

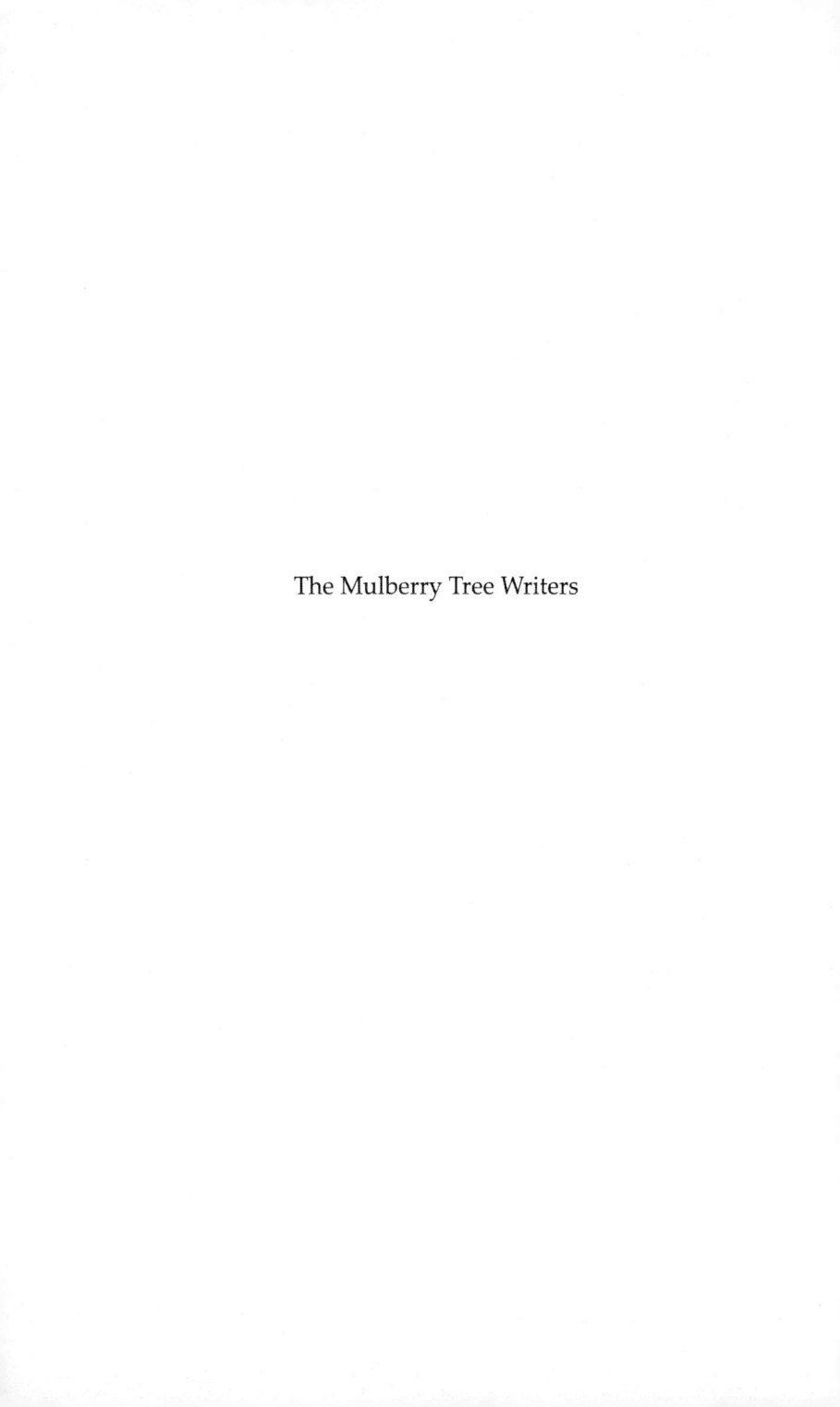

The Mulberry Tree Writers

LEONARD

For five days and five nights Leonard Parker had hardly left his armchair. With the heated chill of fever, he has stayed by the gas fire too unwell even to consider the cost of an energy bill. He spends his nights, mostly indistinguishable from the days, trying to sleep upright in his chair. But the old enemy comes by night as he coughs and wheezes and struggles to catch his breath.

On the sixth day, Leonard feels the fever is past but the chest pains are worse and he knows he must see a doctor. He manages to make an appointment at the Health Centre and begins the slow process of putting on a clean shirt and tie. In the shaving mirror he is shocked by the greyness of the image before him. Leonard is a proud and tidy man. In retirement he has moved from his cottage - 'in the middle of nowhere' as his friends and family were given to calling it - to a modern house on the edge of the small town of Torrington.

For the first time in five days, Leonard draws back the sitting room curtains. He notices the fringes of frost lingering at the edges of the garden path. He hopes the paving will not be slippery. There is a chill to the air as he pulls the front door closed, and the first thing he notices is the empty bird feeder swaying in the breeze. How could he have neglected them so? His concern mounts. Two blue tits fly lower in the branches of the cherry tree as Leonard passes. 'I'll make it up to you all,' he says out loud as he makes his unsteady way down the path. I could have called a taxi, he thinks, but is still functioning on the notion that fresh air would do him good and he'd be better off taking a little exercise.

Leonard

'Dr Hartley has left now Mr Parker,' the receptionist smiles up at Leonard. 'We have Dr Tamworth here as locum until the new doctor comes.'

When Leonard leaves the heat of the Health Centre, he begins to feel very unwell. The tight feeling in his chest is not only due to his respiratory system but more to the unsympathetic attitude of the young doctor who had not even listened to his chest and told him to go the chemist and buy some, as he put it, 'useless bottles of this and that' and that the best thing he can do is to go home and 'carry on coughing'. He is not an aggressive or judgemental man yet anger is in him and he feels near to tears as he turns into the road off the square where he pauses a moment. Should he buy some milk and a newspaper and catch up on the world he has been completely cut off from these days past – he wouldn't be wanting to leave the house again. The shop window startles Leonard with its vibrant red hearts behind the glass. Leonard feels the one in the middle is almost pulsing in its cushion of shiny crimson silk. Happy Valentine's Day is strung across the window in more garish colours. Leonard's own heart aches, he doesn't go into the shop but turns instead down the cobbled alleyway which will act as a short cut and take a few minutes off his weary journey home.

The cobbles are slippery, the morning sun shines bleakly through in places, creating further difficulties for Leonard. He slips slightly and then a rushing sensation is in his head as he stumbles forward to lean against the old stone wall where he tries to catch his breath as the world grows darker and spins around him.

Somewhere a door is pulled open, Leonard remembers hearing the scrape of wood being pulled on stone. A hand on his shoulder guides him steadily, allowing him to leave the safety of the wall. 'You're all done in,' the kind voice says. 'You come on into the warm a while.'

Some days later, when Leonard is recounting the story of the Good Samaritan lady, he tells of how she led him to an armchair with a high back. 'She must have turned up the heating,' he said, 'because the room became very warm.' He told how he started to feel the life coming back into him as she brought him a large mug of tea. At least, he thought it was tea, but something like it anyway, warming his body through and steadying his beating heart.

'You come in any time,' she had told Leonard as she opened the door onto the cobbled alleyway. Leonard thought he remembered a fire glowing and a big black kettle steaming as he turned to thank her. He hadn't even asked her name, he thought as he reached the pathway to his own house. He would go back soon, take some flowers and thank her for what she had done for him.

And one fine March day, one of those days when something changes in the air, when clouds are very white against extra blue skies and open to the sun, Leonard knows it is the right day to make his visit. He picks some daffodils from his garden and sets off towards the square.

The sun is a little higher, the time of day different, so Leonard has reached the end of the alley before realising that he has passed the cottage door. He turns and, without the sun in his eyes, notices for the first time the high chain-link fence on his right. There is a portion left of the old wall Leonard remembers stumbling to hold but, beyond the mesh wire, an empty space where scaffolding is piled and buddleia bushes have pushed through the broken ground. A man in a yellow tin hat is nailing a notice to a post, 'Turner and Pine Construction Engineers'. When Leonard asks the man about the door in the wall and the kind lady's cottage, he says there have been no houses in the lane for ten years or more and they've only just received the go-ahead for the building of new properties because extensive excavation and survey work had to go ahead owing to the instability of the ground, believed by some to be covering plague or leper pits. The man seems willing to talk but Leonard's mind is not taking it all in, his eyes wandering over the bleak site before him where he has seen the shape of an old blue door leaning against a pile of concrete blocks. The door is shaped like a church window. Leonard knows this is the one.

Leonard

'You can't go in there mate,' the man in the yellow hat cautions, but Leonard has already pushed past a gap in the wire fencing and is walking towards the faded blue door. And that is where he carefully lays his yellow daffodils. The man watching removes his daffodil yellow helmet almost in reverence, scratches his head and calls to Leonard. 'Best not stay long in there mate,' he says, 'get me into trouble.'

Leonard smiles and thanks the man. 'I wouldn't want to get anyone into trouble,' he says, and turns down the alley towards the square.

Susan Lyons

***

Angela Nurse

Angela joined the writing group with the intention of recording family memories. Whilst she has written a few personal pieces, she has gained great satisfaction from creating short stories and poems. The natural world and people-watching are her two main inspirations. The talent and skills of the other members of the group have proved a varied and valuable resource to inspire her to improve the quality of her writing. If or when time allows in the future Angela would like to try her hand at a longer piece, maybe even a novel.

AN ATTACHMENT

Anna fastened the ties of her white apron and smoothed it down over the long black skirt of her uniform. She loved her job as a waitress at Lyon's teashop and would miss it immensely once she was married. Her mother's words from earlier that morning echoed in her ears. 'George won't wait forever.' It was a familiar refrain. 'He's a good man, what are you waiting for?'

Anna sighed. She knew George was a good man. They had known each other since childhood. Good, reliable, dependable George. She was very fond of him, she loved him, but it was the same feeling she had for her brothers. George was a friend of one of her elder brothers and ever since he'd asked her to accompany him to a function both of their families had taken it for granted that they were courting. George had a good job as a wages clerk in a local factory and he was sensible with money, he'd saved hard for her pretty little engagement ring. They would be able to continue to save once they were married, as George's mother had offered them her front bedroom, so they would not have to live in digs. But Anna would have to give up her job, married women were not encouraged to continue working at Lyon's teashops and George would want to provide for his wife. So, Anna was putting off setting a date.

Of course there was more to it than just the prospect of setting up home in George's mother's front bedroom. She would feel stifled starting her married life in another woman's home. Anna was naturally outgoing and enjoyed the company of her colleagues and the customers. She would miss the girls she worked with. Sometimes they went to the cinema after work, or occasionally to a dance. Naturally George disapproved, as he was not one for dancing and Anna knew they would never go to a dance together. Their time together was usually spent at home or occasionally having a singsong at the local pub.

However, Anna would miss the customers of the teashop more. The families with young children who would come in for an afternoon ice cream. The lonely people who came in for sticky buns and a pot of tea. The young couples, the older people, Anna knew she would miss them all.

As Anna entered the teashop ready to start her day, the face of one particular customer came into her mind. Alexander's face. He was one of the regular customers and she knew she would miss him the most. He had started coming in for his lunch about a year previously and once their eyes had met Anna had felt an immediate connection. Alexander always chose the same table, so that Anna could serve him. He had an accent, which Anna found charming and in due course she learned that he was Russian. Alexander had left Russia as soon as he could after the revolution and he told her that he lived in one of the big houses overlooking the park. Although, he didn't say much about his life at home, from his comments Anna presumed that he must be a tutor to the children of the house. Whenever time allowed Anna would chat to Alexander while she was serving him, but the manageress of the teashop was strict and was quick to stop too much fraternisation. Frequently Anna noticed Alexander drawing whilst he ate his lunch, and once she thought she caught him sketching her, but he quickly put the sketch book away as she approached.

After a while, sometimes Alexander would wait outside the teashop and offer to walk Anna to her bus stop. Unexpectedly, they had so much to talk about, even though they had so few similarities in their pasts. Alexander was willing to talk about his past life in Russia and his love of art. He told her that he was an artist and had his studio nearby. Anna believed he meant that he liked to draw and paint when he had spare time and he had the space in the big house where he lived. Anna understood that leaving his country of birth after the revolution had been traumatic for him and he had lost or left many friends and family members behind. During their brief periods of time together Anna realised that Alexander's passion for his previous life and his art made a strong contrast to the prospect of life with predictable George. Alexander's stunning good looks and charm were a world away from George's solid presence.

Once, she asked if she could visit his studio but he told her that her reputation was too precious to be tarnished by visiting him alone. Disappointed, but touched by his concern, Anna knew she could be patient.

Over the weeks and months, sometimes Anna would meet Alexander and take her break so they could walk down the river together, but they never walked to the park near where he lived. Anna knew she had fallen in love and believed that Alexander was in love with her too. But he never asked to take her out to the cinema or to see her at the weekend. It was only a few snatched moments here and there. But it was enough, Anna felt alive, she was happy. She lived for those special moments and she knew Alexander did too. Anna wondered if the family he lived with would disapprove of him courting, but she hoped that there might be a chance of life with Alexander.

§

While Anna was contemplating the pressure of commitment to a life with George, a few streets away in the big house overlooking the park, Count Alexander Romanov gazed out of the window, but he was not really looking at the view. Olga came into the room and stood behind him.

'I thought you'd be pleased; the opportunity to paint a different landscape,' she declared.

The opportunity to paint in the South of France was exciting, but Alexander knew he would be leaving his heart behind.

Olga, the daughter of an old family friend had taken him under her wing when he'd arrived from St Petersburg. She supported his art and was now his patron and his wife. It had suited them both at the time. Olga was slightly older than Alexander and was an independent but respectable young woman with connections, which had opened the doors to many people who were prepared to pay for his paintings. Alexander had found a patron to support his work. Olga's friends had purchased his work and he had secured several profitable commissions from an exhibition Olga had arranged for him.

Theirs was a marriage of convenience, but they were happy enough together and planned to honour their commitment to each other. Olga had always organised their lives, but as it had meant that Alexander could paint in peace, he was happy. Or he had been until he met Anna. His painting had taken second place to his enthusiasm to spend as much time with her as he could. He managed to sneak out most days for his lunch, but the time was precious. Now Olga was back in control, she wanted a summer in the South of France. He could not refuse; he'd made his part of the bargain. He had to go. He would have to say goodbye to Anna. It wasn't fair to her, he knew, and there was no future for them.

Later that day Alexander looked through the few pieces of jewellery he'd brought from Russia from his family. He found a tiny gold brooch of a knife, fork and spoon, each holding a tiny pearl and made by the ultimate Russian jewellers, Fabergé. It had been Alexander's mother's brooch, but it would be perfect for his beloved Anna - his soulmate, a waitress at the teashop.

The next day, Alexander met Anna after work and walked her to the bus-stop. Alexander was quieter than normal and Anna realised he had something on his mind. Perhaps he wanted to ask her something. Perhaps her life would be with Alexander. George and both of their families would be upset, but she didn't care.

'Walk with me a little further?' he asked.

They walked on. Anna waited, guessing he had something to say to her. Her heart beat faster. She waited. Eventually they stopped and sat on a bench by the river. Alexander reached into his pocket. He took out the small jewellery box and passed it to her. Anna gasped and looked at him, but he couldn't meet her gaze.

'I'm sorry but I have to go away.' He looked up and into her eyes as they filled with tears.

An Attachment

'Why? Is it the family?' She still believed him to be a tutor from the big house.

'In a way.'

'When will you be back?'

Alexander bit his lip. He couldn't reply, but his silence was the answer. His heart was breaking. He pressed the package into her hand.

'This is for you. I'll never forget you. Remember me.'

§

Many years later.

'Lot 352. A brooch from the Russian jeweller Fabergé: a knife, fork and spoon each with a tiny pearl. Several commission bids, shall we start at one thousand pounds?'

'Two thousand, three.' The auction cards were waving throughout the room.

'Four, five thousand.' Internet bidder.

'Six, six thousand five hundred.' Telephone bids.

'Is there seven anywhere?' One card waved from the back of the room.

The auctioneer's gavel came down. Sold.

Anna's granddaughters had watched the sale and could hardly contain their excitement. They were mystified, how had Grandma Anna owned a Fabergé brooch? Grandad George had never had the money to buy such an exquisite piece of jewellery. Where had it come from? Why had they never seen it before? Why had she kept it?

They could only wonder.

***

Angela Nurse

HEART BEATING

Sunday morning,
Sun shining,
Friends visiting,
Roast cooking,
Pans boiling.

Phone ringing,
Someone talking,
Someone screaming,
Bags packing,
Distance travelling.

Hospital parking,
Resus finding,
Nurses running,
Doctors calling,
Monitors beeping.

Sitting waiting,
Coffee drinking,
Someone praying,
Shadows lengthening,
Clock ticking.

Door opening,
Doctor entering,
Someone sobbing,
Parents grieving,
Forehead kissing.

Heart Beating

Decision making,
Paperwork signing,
Doctors operating,
Organ donating,
Heart beating.

Pagers bleeping,
Phones ringing,
Family travelling,
People hoping,
Doctors operating.

Nurses caring,
Rejection fearing,
Life saving,
Someone smiling,
Future beckoning.

***

SEBASTIAN – ONE DAY IN AUTUMN

Sebastian sat at the breakfast table, picking dejectedly at the bacon and egg in front of him. Even though it was presented beautifully on fine china, it still didn't tempt his appetite. He did not like eggs, but tradition dictated that bacon and egg were served for breakfast at home. He much preferred toast and jam or porridge that was provided when he was at school. In fact on reflection he preferred almost everything about school to life at home. It was half term and usually during the holidays he would visit school chums or one of them would come to stay with him. But this week, nothing had been planned and he was stuck at home without entertainment.

Sebastian's mother was flicking through a fashion magazine whilst picking daintily at the bowl of fruit in front of her. She looked glamorous and immaculate as always. Some of the boys at school thought she was beautiful, which was really embarrassing as most of them had mothers who looked like proper mothers.

Sebastian's father was tucking into his full plate of breakfast with great enthusiasm, whilst engrossed in his newspaper. Reaching the end of an article, father folded the newspaper.

'So young man, what are your plans for today? Your mother and I are off to an auction in Templeton.'

Sebastian shrugged, realising that he would be left alone all day. Much as he was tempted to say 'Dunno', as some of the boys at school might, he knew his father would react angrily.

'I don't know yet, Father,' he replied.

'Any homework? How about piano practice?' his father enquired.

Sebastian sighed inwardly and said. 'Maybe I could take Dolly out for a ride.'

Dolly, the pony from Sebastian's childhood was a great favourite, but Sebastian knew she was too small for him now.

'Ask Trentham to find something more suitable for you if you want to ride, old chap,' replied his father.

'Yes, Father.' Sebastian hid a smile, at least now he had approval to get out of the house.

Riding was not Sebastian's favourite activity, but it would mean being outside and he could wear old trousers and a comfy sweater. Sebastian was happy. After breakfast was cleared away and his parents had departed, Sebastian went to change his clothes. Mrs Trentham, the cook/housekeeper was cleaning in the hallway.

'Morning Mr Sebastian.'

'Oh, Mrs T, please just call me Seb like you used to.'

'You know your parents wouldn't like that.'

'They're not here,' he smiled giving her a hug.

'Did you enjoy your breakfast,' she asked.

'I'd rather have porridge or toast and jam like we do at school.'

'You and your sweet tooth,' Mrs T smiled. 'Come downstairs in a minute and I'll get you some.'

Sebastian smiled and gave her another big hug, not something he ever did to his parents. The day was improving already. A few minutes later, Sebastian and Mrs T were sitting together in the warm, cosy kitchen. Sebastian had changed into his old clothes and his wellingtons were by the back door.

'Were you planning to go riding?' Mrs T asked, 'only Mr T has just gone into town and won't be back until this afternoon.'

'That's OK, I'd rather go to the woods anyway.'

'Joy is in the cottage,' hinted Mrs T, 'she'd be pleased to see you.'

Sebastian and Joy had played together frequently as small children, but since Sebastian had been away at school they had not seen much of each other. Sebastian hesitated, he knew his parents would not be pleased, they were encouraging him to move in different circles now. However, if he didn't go with Joy, he knew he would not be allowed to go to the woods on his own.

'Go and give her a knock and I'll pack you some sandwiches.'

As predicted, Joy was delighted to see her old friend and once she donned her boots and a thick sweater, they were ready. Handing the children their lunch in an old knapsack, Mrs T reminded them to be back by 4 o'clock.

'Come back through Long Acre field and see if there are any mushrooms on the ridge.'

As country children, they knew that the big flatcaps which grew along the ridge in Long Acre field would be delicious and Sebastian thought that maybe they would be for tomorrow's breakfast rather than the hated bacon and egg.

The children set off and headed uphill through the woods. Stopping frequently, they watched squirrels rushing busily up and down the trees and burying nuts in the soft leaf mould. Sebastian and Joy decided to help and gathered a pile of acorns and left them at the bottom of the tree ready for the squirrels.

Next they decided to have a biggest leaf/smallest leaf competition and passed the time happily collecting the brightly coloured specimens. Having declared that event a draw, they carried on through the woods. Suddenly, as one, they stopped. Ahead of them on the path, a large stag was standing proudly and looking haughtily at them. The children froze, knowing the slightest movement would send him dashing for cover. The stag eyed the children with a superior look, then bored with them, he set off through the woods and was soon in deep cover.

'Wow, what a beauty,' Joy whispered. Both children were thrilled with their rare glimpse of the stag.

At the top of the hill the woodland cleared to provide a viewpoint of the valley and the village. The children sat on an old tree trunk and ate their lunch, wishing there were more to eat. Below they could see activity down on the village green.

'Let's go there next,' suggested Sebastian.

'Ok, race you,' Joy replied and dashed off downhill back through the woods.

Within a few minutes they arrived in the village and collapsed puffing in a heap together by the green.

'I won,' laughed Sebastian, 'even though you cheated with a head start.'

'It's not fair,' replied Joy 'you're taller than me now.'

'How about I buy you a sticky bun?' Sebastian was already on his feet and heading towards the village bakery.

'Yummy,' replied Joy, 'what are we waiting for?'

Buns purchased, the children sat on a bench under a horse chestnut tree.

'Delicious,' remarked Joy, licking her slightly grubby fingers.

'Who can find the biggest conker?'

'Bet I can.'

Sadly there weren't many good conkers to be found. The children from the village must have been out earlier in the day and collected all the good ones.

Their attention turned to the activity that they had spotted from the top of the hill. A big bonfire was being built ready for the 5th of November. Now they were close up, the children could see that it was enormous and several local people were gathered around, chatting and bringing more wood for the fire.

'Penny for the guy?' a little voice piped up.

Sebastian threw a couple of coins into the cup offered. The guy was a half-hearted attempt, with an outfit of faded, threadbare men's pyjamas, a paper bag for a face and a hat made from shiny brown paper, no doubt begged from the little boy's mother who must have been using it for ironing. Joy looked up at the clock on the church.

'We'd better head home if we are to be back by four, especially if we are going to look for mushrooms,' reminded Joy.

'Ooh yes, come on, I want mushrooms for breakfast tomorrow.'

The children set off and in Long Acre field, as hoped, they found several big mushrooms and delivered them to Mrs T shortly before 4 o'clock.

'Look at the state of you both,' scolded Mrs T. 'Go and get yourselves cleaned up.' Joy headed home and Sebastian dashed upstairs, washed his hands and face and changed his clothes.

Back downstairs, Mrs T brought him a cup of tea and a big slice of fruitcake.

'Now how about that piano practice?' she reminded.

***

Angela Nurse

IT'S NOT 'ARRODS

A buzz of excitement as I walk through the door,
What is it exactly that I'm looking for?

New trousers, a CD, a dress or a book,
That's part of the fun, you don't know till you look.

Like a child in a sweet-shop, the temptation's there,
Something for the house, or something to wear.

To part with my cash, whilst buying new treasures,
Is it consumerism, or one of life's pleasures.

The Red Cross, The Dog's Trust, I'm not worried where,
It's all for good causes, they need us to care.

I admit it, I'm hooked, I keep going back,
Sometimes to donate stuff, wrapped up in a sack.

So this week, I'll pop in, I can't stay away,
You just never know what you might find today.

GILLIAN JONES

As usual Gillian awoke before the alarm sounded and immediately her thoughts turned to the day ahead. 'Here goes,' she thought to herself, 'it's only one day.'

Throwing on old jeans and a fleece she grabbed a coffee from the kitchen and headed out to the stables to her beloved horses. Once they were all fed and watered and fussed over, she turned them out into one of the paddocks and headed back indoors. Another coffee, whilst Gillian prepared herself a hearty breakfast, fruit, porridge and scrambled eggs on toast. Gillian wasn't sure how long it would be before she would be able to eat again today, so she wanted to have a good start. She sprinkled cinnamon on her porridge. She'd read somewhere that it was good for you, but she couldn't remember why. Despite her nerves, Gillian managed her breakfast and headed back upstairs to prepare for the day.

'Don't be silly,' she told herself, 'you've done days like today, hundreds of times before.'

'Yes, but it was 40 years ago,' came her own reply.

As a famous model in the 1960s, Gillian Jones was a super model long before the description existed. She'd been known as JillyJo and her strawberry blond hair, pale skin, green eyes and tall, willowy frame had been famous the world over. Even after her marriage to Jim Prentice, the lead singer in the rock band Tempus Fugit, she was only ever known professionally as JillyJo.

During the sixties, Gillian travelled the world and worked long demanding hours in order to be recognised for some of the iconic fashion shoot photos from the period. JillyJo's career continued into the seventies and eighties at a more manageable level as the face of a prestigious cosmetics brand.

JillyJo was loved by the generation of women who had grown up with her and tried to look after their appearance. Whilst men found her attractive, she'd been promoted with an image of the girl next door and that provided a more enduring career.

JillyJo retired from modelling in the nineties and with their son, now grown-up and living in Australia, Gillian had found time to indulge her passion for horses. As a successful couple, Gillian and Jim were able to afford a magnificent house deep in the Surrey countryside, with land for her horses. Despite the rural life they had chosen, they were close enough to London and its travel links, for their careers. As the years progressed, Gillian developed her love of horses into a rescue charity to which she was now devoted. Gillian never played on her success as JillyJo for her charity, she preferred it to be all about the horses.

At the age of 67, the offer of a photo shoot and Christmas advertising campaign for a major high street store had come out of the blue for JillyJo. The campaign was to feature women of all ages, many famous from years before and the idea was to recreate some iconic shots from the past, but wearing the current season's clothing range by the retailer. It had taken a while for her to decide whether she wanted to face the whole modelling circus again. However, the money offered was too good to turn down and she thought of the horses that she would be able to help. Gillian was desperate to buy more land in order to expand the rescue charity in another part of the country.

With Jim's encouragement, Gillian agreed to go to the initial meetings, and once she met some of the other women involved, her confidence increased. As a result of her pale complexion, and burning easily, Gillian had always looked after her skin and felt more confident with her own appearance particularly once she saw one of the other models, an ageing actress, who looked like a little old lady without her makeup and designer clothes.

So JillyJo agreed and in the end she thoroughly enjoyed the photo shoot. She was pleased with the photos to be used and whilst she found the video of the TV commercial embarrassing, overall she found that it boosted her confidence.

So today, the big day, the launch of the advertising campaign. The event was to be held as a lunchtime event at the Grand Connaught Rooms in London. The first time Gillian would be seen in public as JillyJo for over twenty years. She needed to look her best. The store would be providing clothes, hair and make-up for the launch, but she wanted to feel good. Although she knew it was very unlikely she would be recognised prior to the event, she would need more than hair scraped back and minimal make-up.

Gillian headed back into the bedroom with a cup of tea for Jim who was just stirring.

'It's not too late,' he said. 'I can come with you if you wish. Moral support.'

'No, don't worry,' Gillian replied. 'I'll be fine, it would be so boring for you. All that talk about clothes and fashion.'

'All those glamorous women!' he replied with a grin. 'I don't think I'd be bored, but I don't want to spoil your day. I'll look forward to hearing all about it later.'

With the continued success of Jim's band, he'd be instantly recognisable and the tabloids would love the photo opportunity and chance to question their long and happy marriage. However, Gillian knew she was working today and it was all about the publicity for the company's campaign.

An hour later, happy with her appearance, smart jeans, white top and navy blazer, with her still long strawberry blond hair styled in a casual side plait. Gillian left the house.

Once she'd driven to the small local station and was waiting on the platform, Gillian took a few deep breaths. The last clean fresh air she'd breathe for the rest of the day. As the train approached, with one last deep breath to calm her nerves, Gillian pulled herself up straight and with her posture correct JillyJo was ready.

The train pulled into Waterloo on time and Gillian took a cab to the Grand Connaught Rooms. Normally she would have been quite happy to take the tube, but today she wanted to arrive feeling calm and composed.

Once welcomed by the styling team, she settled down to have her hair redone and her simple make-up removed. It was decided that JillyJo was to wear the outfit from one of the campaign's photo shoots, which it was hoped would capture the public's imagination. The photo had recreated an iconic sixties photo of JillyJo standing on Waterloo Bridge with Big Ben in the background and a London bus passing by. In the sixties photo JillyJo wore a mini dress, in a green paisley print, with long boots known as kinky boots at the time. Green was the colour that had always suited her best, even though many of the original photos had been produced in black and white. Gosh, it all seemed such a long time ago; so much had changed. So the new photo almost exactly re-created the original. This time JillyJo was dressed in a green paisley tunic, but with skinny jeans and chunky boots. Still a good look, but contemporary and appropriate for her age. A huge relief to Gillian.

Chatting to some of the other women, modelling for the campaign, they were all apprehensive of the new approach of using older women. But they were all real women, they liked to look good never mind their age.

Time for the launch. JillyJo was pleased for her previous experience. She knew how to behave at these events and knew better than to eat anything whilst there were photographers present and she stuck to sparking water in her champagne flute. Meanwhile the media had arrived and were tucking into the canapés, washed down with as much champagne as they wanted.

Gillian observed the fashion journalists air kissing each other and squealing with false delight at seeing each other. The environment hadn't been so bitchy in the past.

This was it, the moment of truth. The CEO of the company welcomed the guests, and then the photo stills were presented to the assembled crowd. There were a few gasps and ripples of applause as some of the shots were displayed. At the end of the stills, the TV commercial was shown. JillyJo had to admit to herself: it looked OK. At the end of the presentation, there was tremendous applause and the CEO introduced the models to the audience. More applause. JillyJo felt good and had a huge sense of relief. The media liked it. There would be good reviews of the store's collection in the press. It would only be deemed a true success if sales of the items were increased, but there seemed to be a good vibe in the room. The first showing would be at prime time on TV the following evening.

Then it was time to work the room, chat to journalists, promote the clothes, trying to discourage personal questions whilst still charming the crowd.

At last the event was over, back to the styling team to take off the heavy make-up and change back into her jeans and jacket. As Gillian had expected she was allowed to keep her clothes from the event. Not that she'd be wearing them herself, but she might be able to auction the outfit for her charity.

It had been quite an occasion, a reminder of her previous life. The attention, the venues, the styling, the recognition meant that JillyJo had enjoyed herself enormously. In the taxi returning to the station, the taxi driver smiled at Gillian.

'How's your day, darling?'

'Like stepping back in time.'

He looked puzzled, but she didn't expand. Back at Waterloo, Gillian scanned the departure's board for her train. It was rush hour now and the crowds were building. Anonymous once more, she smiled to herself as she found a seat for the journey home.

'How did it go?' Jim was waiting for Gillian as she arrived home. 'Cup of tea?'

'I'd love one, thanks. Put the kettle on and I'll tell you all about it.'

***

Angela Nurse

YOU WON'T REMEMBER ME

I wasn't the eldest child, I wasn't the youngest one,
I wasn't the only girl, or just the only son,
I wasn't the one with curly hair,
You won't remember me.

I wasn't top of the class, yet nor was I the dunce,
I didn't win any prizes, not expelled even once,
I wasn't good at music or sports,
You won't remember me.

I wasn't very pretty, I wasn't very tall,
I wasn't really ugly, I wasn't rather small,
I wasn't fat or really thin,
You won't remember me.

I wasn't at all famous, but I think I did succeed,
I didn't become a vagrant, I wasn't one in need,
I wasn't controversial,
You won't remember me.

I didn't see my name in lights, I wasn't on the stage,
I didn't invent something new, but yet I earned a wage,
I didn't discover the cure for colds,
You won't remember me.

I studied and passed and then I worked, I bought a little house,
I loved and married just the once, we really meant our vows,
My spouse's mind left a while ago,
He can't remember me.

I grew old and had grey hair, my bones began to ache,
Just like all the others, who have left me in their wake,
One by one they left this earth,
They won't remember me.

If one day you read this poem, see my name in black and white,
You hear my voice and pause, that sounds just right,
I wasn't very memorable, but,
You will remember me.

THE POPPIES

They went to war when they were boys,
They didn't really have a choice.

They marched away and looked so brave,
While mothers and sweethearts smiled and waved.

Was it Cyril or Tom or Bert,
Who left to fight, they'd not get hurt.

They were sent to Belgium and France,
They didn't really stand a chance.

So patriotic and filled with pride,
But within each regiment, young men died.

A bright red poppy, became the sign,
For remembrance of that time.

One year, ceramic ones were made,
Each one unique, and people paid

To raise money and honour the men,
Who were never seen again.

And then each poppy, crafted by hand,
Was displayed at the Tower for people to stand

and look in awe, and some shed tears,
For what was lost during those years.

In the moat, a sea of red,
Not blood this time, though men were dead.

Eight hundred thousand and more were lost,
So many lives and such a cost.

One poppy, one man, so many died,
Who was your link, your family's pride?

Angela Nurse

THE BEACH HUT

It's only a shed, so some people say,
To me it's a palace overlooking the bay.

With white picket fence and painted bright blue,
The perfect location to enjoy the view.

Inside, full of charm as cute as can be,
With bunting and cushions and space to make tea.

There's storage for wellies, umbrellas and macs,
And buckets and spades are placed up on racks.

The waves rolling in, the sparkling sea,
Glitters and glistens, a great place to be.

My place to retreat, my refuge from life,
To rest, to be still, escape all the strife.

A place to relax and enjoy the sun,
Indian summer, at last it's begun.

I'll visit alone to savour the peace,
Or take all the girls for cake and for teas.

To sit and to stare, to lick an ice-cream,
Or gaze into space and sometimes day-dream.

The Beach Hut

In winter, a shelter from dark brooding skies,
In spring, if I'm early I'll watch the sunrise.

In summer, the shade, from scorching hot sun,
In autumn, the memories of times filled with fun.

To look at the view and sit on a bench,
And watch some small children start digging a trench.

To bury their dad, right down to his toes,
Then run off and leave him, while he has a doze.

The tide's coming in, oh no he'll get wet,
The children are laughing, the greatest fun yet.

The end of the day, it's time to go home,
And so that is the end of this little poem.

***

KATIE'S COTTAGE/BWTHYN CATRIN

Katie knew she was almost at her destination as she turned into the narrow lane heading toward the sea. Not far now and she would arrive at the tiny cottage. It had taken her four hours to drive to Pembrokeshire from her home in the Midlands, and she was glad her journey was at an end. She wasn't sure that she wanted to be there really, but she knew that she needed to visit the cottage in order to be certain. It had come as a complete surprise on her 25th birthday, when Katie discovered that she had inherited the property in a trust set up by her late Great Aunt Catrin. At 25, Katie was concerned about the responsibility of the upkeep of an old building which was miles away from her home. The small house had been let out for holidays for many years until finally Katie inherited it. Katie could barely remember her Great Aunt. She recalled that they visited her once at this cottage when Katie was a small child and her family were on holiday in Tenby. Her only memory was of the formidable old lady offering tea and Welsh cakes which were cooked on the griddle over the fire. As a finicky child Katie was horrified, it was like barbecuing indoors, which she knew was not allowed.

Now, the cottage belonged to Katie and although her instinct was to sell it in order to provide a deposit to buy her own home, Katie's parents insisted that she visit Pembrokeshire before she decided. They wanted to accompany her, but she chose to visit alone, to make up her own mind. Katie was surprised to learn that Great Aunt Catrin was not a spinster, as she thought, but had been married to a Welshman and had a son. Sadly they both died whilst Catrin was still quite young and she remained alone in the little cottage for the rest of her life.

So, here she was. Katie had arrived at Bwthyn Catrin. She parked her car on the rough grass at the front and looked at the cottage that was now hers. She was going to try to keep an open mind. The old stone building stood solidly in front of her. It looked tiny from the outside, even smaller than she remembered. Made of local stone, with a grey slate roof and one tiny window facing the front. Yes, Katie knew all about tiny windows and thick walls for insulation, but she was sure it would be dark and gloomy inside. She reached for the key and opened the solid front door. The cold air rushed out to greet her. The late sun of the day had not permeated inside at all. Katie went back to the car and put on her jacket. Back inside again, she left the front door open, hoping for some of the last warmth of the day to trickle in. The front door led straight into the living room. This one room would have been the extent of the original cottage and was the room Katie remembered from her visit as a child. A second tiny window facing west welcomed the fading sunlight and reflected the warm tone of the stone walls. The open fire, which had heated the griddle Katie remembered, was gone and a chunky pot-bellied stove stood in the fireplace. Small as the little house was, above Katie's head there was a crog loft, where the original occupants would have slept. Now the loft was purely decorative, as it had been deemed too dangerous for use by the holidaymakers.

Katie dug into the pocket of her jacket and took out the letter from the solicitors. She read through the instructions and quickly moved through from the living room to the kitchen and located the stopcock and the fuse box, so that she could turn on the water and power. Outside the light was beginning to fade and soon it would be dark and cold. Why did she decline the electric fan heater that her sensible mother suggested she bring?

The kitchen, small but not minute. This room had been added about 100 years previously and Katie found it less oppressive than the living room. It was a galley style kitchen, but very dated with old-fashioned cupboards and a window looking out at the small side garden. The window was larger than the tiny ones in the living room and also enjoyed the last of the sun's rays. The cottage was still furnished and equipped with all the necessities for the holidaymakers who had rented the property over the years since Great Aunt Catrin passed away. The rental income had been used for essential repairs and costs, but Katie knew there was also a sum of money in the trust, which was now hers.

Everything seemed dated and shabby to Katie. However, it was clean and although she decided to boil the kettle a couple of times and wash the utensils before she used them, it was OK.

From the kitchen Katie passed though into a narrow corridor into the 1960s extension at the back of the cottage. A small shower room, complete with a hideous sludgy green coloured suite. Katie had heard of the infamous avocado bathroom suite, but never seen one before. Well, it was almost retro she thought with a smile. The three bedrooms were at the back. One small narrow room, with bunk beds. The second slightly larger with just room for a double bed and a chest of drawers. Hooks on a plank were provided for hanging clothes. Katie quite liked that feature. Shabby chic. The third bedroom was right at the back of the property. It was slightly larger and with a lovely big window which overlooked the rear garden. Well, open space rather than garden. It was just grass, easy to maintain and space for families with children to play. The boundary seemed to comprise of a bank of earth topped by some wispy green shrubs, common by the sea, but Katie didn't know what they were called.

Part of Katie wanted to take photos, send them to her friends, laugh at the avocado bathroom suite and the old-fashioned electric cooker in the kitchen but something stopped her. Some friends had wanted to accompany her on the visit to the cottage, keen for her to keep it, no doubt with their own interests for free holidays in mind. Katie felt slightly defensive now she had arrived. At one time this little house was her Great Aunt's home.

Heading back through to the kitchen Katie switched on the one night storage heater in the corridor. There would be no heat today, but maybe it would be warmer in the morning. In the kitchen, Katie emptied and refilled the kettle, then went out to the car and brought in her bags. The sun had set and it was really chilly now. She switched on the oven and opened the door, hoping that it would warm her up. She walked back to the living room and looked at the pot bellied stove, with a basket of logs beside it. What was she supposed to do with that? Katie peered inside and noticed that it had been set ready for lighting. What a relief. She took the box of matches and lit a piece paper at the bottom. It caught and the fire started to burn. Why wasn't she warm yet?

As night fell, slowly the cottage began to warm up. Katie made herself beans on toast and another cup of tea and realised that she would have to make up one of the beds and brave the chill in the bathroom and the bedroom.

Katie chose the largest room at the back of the cottage and piled the duvet and all the blankets she could find onto the bed and filled the hot water bottle she had found in one of the cupboards. She hoped it wouldn't burst but it was heaven to snuggle up to. Outside the weather had taken a turn for the worse and the wind was blowing and rain was lashing at the window. Exhaustion eventually took over and Katie slept.

***

Ann Thomas

Ann Thomas enjoyed writing stories at school and essays in later studies. During her working life she mainly wrote reports for her work which she feels assisted her in organising facts and giving clear descriptions, as well as overall views of situations. She occasionally wrote short articles for community and parish magazines. Retirement brought the opportunity to do more writing and to be more creative in short stories and poetry using both fact and fiction.

SPRINGTIME IN THE GARDEN

Marion found the painting. She thought it would be in the exhibition, which was a retrospective of Gerald Llewellyn's work up to recent times.

The picture had been painted so long ago. It was in pale, muted colours and more like a print – a cross between a watercolour and an etching. But Gerald had been an illustrator and had rarely brought bright primary colours into his work.

Marion half smiled in memory and in sadness. She doubted whether anyone in the room would know it was a portrait of herself and her older cousin, Celia, sitting in their garden on a warm afternoon in late spring. It looks tranquil, Celia with her book and herself leaning back after just shelling peas, but this was a time of anxiety as the date was 1942 and the country was at war.

Marion's thoughts went back to those days. She had thought of them frequently over the years, but then always tried to push them to the back of her mind. Today, however, she could do no other than to face them again and maybe, she thought, this could be a way, to some degree, to come to terms with it all. She brushed a tear from her eye – oh, if only she had known what was to come.

Marion and Celia had been left a large house in the Suffolk countryside, not far from the village of Thorpe Green, by a mutual uncle, just before the Second World War. They did not know what to do with it at first but, when the war began, they decided to keep it, at least for the time being, and to run it as a guest house for military and people displaced by war from their homes and occupations to that area of Suffolk.

Celia had been a secretary in London and her firm had closed down. Her only alternative then was to return to her parents in Scotland. Marion, who only had her father now, and he was cared for by her brother and his wife, had worked in catering for business events and had lived in Reading.

So now they decided to keep themselves going by taking in guests. Some were with them for longer periods than others. They were fortunate also in supporting themselves by having a reasonably large garden given over mainly to fruit and vegetables. They were helped in this by Stanley Jones, a retired gardener who lived nearby.

Among their guests were several groups of military officers who each stayed a number of weeks and Joan and Sally, the wife and daughter of David, who worked in Whitehall in London. Their home had been destroyed in the bombings. David remained in London, but Joan and Sally stayed in Suffolk for quite a long time.

David made weekend visits when he could, but he never spoke about what he was doing or what was happening in London. Sally and Joan were so pleased to see him on these occasions and, apart from spending time at the house, they went for walks or a rare trip to the cinema in the nearby town.

Joan had made herself useful by helping with voluntary work in the village, raising funds for the war effort through regular jumble sales, helping with meals, knitting garments from reusable wool and collecting items for parcels to send to the troops. She occasionally did small things for Marion and Celia when they were busy.

Sally had quite taken to the small country school and soon made friends, especially with Shirley, a girl of her own age who lived nearby and they spent time together after school which pleased Joan for she felt Sally might by lonely after leaving London.

It was towards the end of 1941 when Celia took a telephone call from the Ministry of Agriculture to ask if they could put up a member of their department, but gave no other details. As a room was free, and guests had to show their identity cards and personal credentials, Celia accepted the booking.

Two days later Gerald Llewellyn arrived at their door. He was a tall, quite distinguished looking man with dark hair and contrasting pale blue eyes. Celia later described him to Marion who was in the kitchen preparing an evening meal. 'Do you think he is an inspector of any kind?' she added. 'Well, maybe he's to do with farming or something similar,' her cousin replied.

When she met him, Marion was struck by one thing, and that was how a forelock of dark hair formed a large curl which twisted in the opposite direction to the main lie of his hair. A silly thing to notice, she thought.

Gerald, they discovered, was an illustrator and was fairly well known before the war, mainly for his work for books and magazines and sometimes for newspapers. With his particular interest in wildlife, he had a great knowledge of animals and plants. They eventually learnt he had been asked by the Ministry of Agriculture to assess the situation in parts of East Anglia in regard to the use of land for food production and the effect this could be having on the countryside and wildlife.

Gerald usually spent the whole day away, sometimes cycling around the area, occasionally taking his rather old car if it was possible to get petrol, to more distant places. When he came in he would often pop his head around the kitchen door to ask how their day had gone, and they gradually got to know him.

Showing an interest in wildlife, Celia would ask Gerald about things he drew, for he continued with some of his illustration work while staying with them, some in support of his present work. It was then he asked if he could paint them in the garden one warm, late spring afternoon, and this was what Marion saw before her now.

On occasions he would come into their sitting room and talk with them for a while. Celia was an eager listener and talker, while Marion would sit more quietly, often mending garments or knitting items for the war effort. However, she listened and was eager to learn new things. There were times, on a rare day off, when he would invite them both, if they were free, to walk to the nearby village and have a drink at the Haymakers' Inn. He felt it was good for them to get out a little and have a change.

On the way he would point out various things in the landscape, especially the plants. Marion began to notice how Celia became quite animated when Gerald was around and Celia said she really liked the slight Welsh lilt in his voice – he came from Montgomeryshire.

When Autumn arrived Gerald sometimes had to go to London for a few days regarding his work. On one particular occasion Celia had an appointment there at the same time and Gerald was quite happy for her to travel with him. They would take the car to Stowmarket and then the train to London. Celia then arranged for a friend to pick her up at the railway station from the evening train. Jenny, who lived nearby, would come in to help Marion if she needed her, as she often did on some occasions.

Jenny was reliable. She lived in a cottage a short walk down the lane from the house. Her husband, Stan, was in the Army and she worried about him. She was a concerned mother and a good worker. With a girl, Shirley, and two boys, Peter and Clive, all of school age to look after on her own, she was very grateful for any extra work she could get apart from her regular cleaning jobs at several houses in the village.

She had an evacuee for a while, a young boy, Roger, who had been separated from his family during bombing in London, but fortunately his family was found and he went to join his older brother billeted in the West Country. Jenny always enjoyed working for the 'two ladies' as she called them and, knowing her circumstances, Marion often gave her any spare food if she had it.

Marion was in bed when Celia returned and didn't see her until the following morning, when she felt Celia seemed rather quiet. She knew she had to go to London on some business, but Celia was fairly non-committal when Marion asked her how her day had gone. She supposed Celia was tired and London was not really the place to be in these anxious times.

A few days later Celia received a telephone call from her father in Scotland. Her mother was unwell and he asked her to come home for a few days. She felt she ought to go and so it was arranged for Jenny to come in more often if Marion needed her. (Although Marion said she could manage as there were only six guests at present, including Joan and Sally who had settled in and almost completely looked after themselves.)

Several days later Gerald rang up to say he would be back the following evening and asked how they both were. Marion told him Celia had gone to Scotland.

When Gerald arrived he seemed pleased to see Marion and the other guests. He described London as being a nightmare with several air raids during his stay and that he was glad to be back. Celia then telephoned to say she was going to have to stay longer than expected, but Marion assured her she would manage.

On her own, Marion began to talk more easily to Gerald. Often they spoke in the kitchen in the evening while the others came in and out to make drinks and find biscuits. One evening Gerald told Marion his plan of work would be over in a few months. 'Can't make it any longer I'm afraid,' he said with a sad smile. Then he went on to say he had been seriously thinking of joining up and would probably be expected to do so as his 'essential work', as his job had been called, would be over. This would be about Springtime. He revealed he had no close family and felt he ought to 'do his bit' as he put it, 'for the country'.

Marion had very mixed feelings about this news but knew how patriotism was encouraged at times like these. Gerald said he hoped he might join the Army Medical Corps. He had in fact studied for two years for a medical degree before changing his mind for art and illustration instead. He said, half jokingly, 'I found Leonardo's drawings and those in Gray's Anatomy much more interesting than studying medicine, but I do know a few things and could be of some help I'm sure.'

Celia came back towards the end of February and heard the news that Gerald was due to leave them in early March. He had signed up for the Army. They had wanted him to be an officer in the General Army but he persuaded them to let him join the Medical Corps. Then after training, he would be posted abroad.

Celia was quieter with him now, although he was always kind to her. The day he left was painful for them all, but he promised to write. Both Celia and Marion missed him very much indeed. Somehow it was as if a light had gone out of their lives, but although saddened, they continued with their work.

However, as the days passed, Marion was finding it much harder to cope with the work, she seemed to do more of the heavier, physical work than Celia. Her doctor then recommended she should take a break for a short while. She decided to go to her brother, who was in a reserved occupation, and his wife in Dorset for a week or two while Jenny helped Celia at home.

While Marion was away, two letters came from Gerald. Celia was delighted, but also rather puzzled as one letter was for her and the other for Marion. His letter told Celia he was well but not much about his situation, which she knew would be censored of course. He spoke mainly about their walks and the wildlife he had enjoyed seeing in Thorpe Green and wished her well. Celia again wondered why a separate letter to Marion? Then, overcome by curiosity, she steamed it open and read it. Her face changed. She looked angry and then she tore it up and threw it away.

On top of this, Marion wrote to Celia two days later to say her family needed her to stay on for a while longer. This annoyed Celia and she decided she could not carry on alone, so she wrote to tell Marion she was going to close up the house and suggested they sell it as soon as possible once the war was over. She made no mention of Gerald.

All this Marion remembered so well. She had not moved from in front of the picture.

Marion had remained with her family in Dorset after Celia's letter and eventually found a home there herself. Celia did as she had said. She closed the house and returned to Scotland. Marion received no news of Gerald and, for some reason, Celia had refused to speak about him. The house remained closed and was sold, as agreed, towards the end of 1945. Marion then lost touch with Celia who never contacted her again.

Springtime in the Garden

Marion had tried to find out what had happened to Gerald when the war was over but to no avail. Then, several years later, she heard through an Army friend of her family, that it was thought Gerald had been caught up in an attack and had died in 1944, which brought her great sadness. Then a few years later she heard this was not true. He had been badly wounded but had survived and after a while had married, but there were no children.

He continued with his illustration work when he was well enough, but it had become much darker in mood and time than his work of earlier years. At the exhibition there were some war sketches lent by the Imperial War Museum and this darker mood was very evident in these.

Gerald had died several years ago and his widow, Margaret, who was several years older than him, died in the past year. Instructions were left in her will that an exhibition of Gerald's life's work should be produced and a particular picture 'Springtime in the Garden,' was to be given to Miss Marion Johns when the exhibition ended.

So it was to come to her after all. Marion had received a letter placed with Margaret's will. In it Margaret said she knew how good Marion had been to Gerald and he had written to her from abroad but had never received a reply. Although he looked for her after the war ended, he could not find her, but he requested that somehow she should have the Springtime picture.

Marion wiped away the tears that came again and then turned around to look at her son, who seemed mesmorised by the wildlife illustrations on the opposite wall. Cap in hand, he looked handsome in his RAF uniform which echoed the colour of his blue eyes and complimented his dark hair with the forelock that twisted into a curl in the opposite direction to which his hair lay.

WEDDING

How chance was it to meet?
Or was it chance we say,
That led us down the winding path
Towards this Happy Day.

You stand before me now
In crown of white, a bride,
I look at you and see
A sweet and gentle face
Who caused me many sighs.

We met, becoming friends
And agreed just friends to stay.
But came a time for me
When I had more to say.

Yet truth to tell, not once but twice
You smiled and shook your head
Maybe too, as scared as me
You feared what might be said.

I walked alone to think things through,
For a time I stayed that way
Then I decided just once more, to try,
And if you still said 'Nay',
I'd say goodbye
And take my heart a million miles away.

Wedding

But love won through and you said 'yes',
　　Much to my great delight.
　Now both of us had learned to trust
　　And face a future bright.

And now with this gold ring we wed,
　　A band to truly say
　For good or ill we share our lives
　　For ever and a day.

　And now we celebrate this time
　　With family and friends.
　　And feelings mixed we all
　Must feel as a new phase starts
　　And an old one ends.

So down the winding path we've come
　　And through the gate at last,
　And on to unknown pastures new
　　Our two hands tightly clasped.

***

THROUGH THE RAINBOW

Recently as I was sorting through some bags of newspaper cuttings and items of interest from magazines I had stored away some time ago, I came across a broadsheet newspaper cutting of 1999. It was about a personal condition that affects around four percent of the population and some people are not even aware they have it.

It is an inherited condition through the female line and more women have it than men. I am interested as I have this condition to some degree. The article assures the reader that it is not a psychiatric condition and there is no treatment for it.

The tone of the article implies it is a medical condition which the writer suggests is a burden to those who have it. I find this attitude of the reporter rather amusing as, although it is unusual, it does not really disadvantage the 'sufferers' as he calls us, rather in some ways it can be an advantage.

The condition is synaesthesia, where the pathways in the brain are wired differently from the norm, so that some of the senses become cross-activated. I think, as long as I can remember, I have seen colours around numbers and letters and in fact I assumed everybody had this ability. I see a black written letter, say 'A' and around it will be a halo of colour rather as if a water colour wash had been painted over it. Some people see music in colour, and some even taste.

It happens, it is said, when different parts of the brain involved in perception are too close to each other. Novelist Caroline Vermalle, is a synaethesic who has researched it more and she wrote an interesting magazine article about it recently. She has grapheme-colour synaesthesia, the most common form, which I believe is my type also. She sees the condition as a gift and not a negative experience, as some more scientifically-minded people might do, and I agree with her.

Just as Caroline does, I see colours around numbers zero to nine and each letter of the alphabet. The colours are always the same for the same letters and numbers, but where I see a particular colour for the letter 'A', someone else might always see a different colour from mine. Also, for me, names particularly and words can have a block colour or blend of colours around them. I find this ability useful in remembering such things as my PIN numbers and I always see these when I use a cash or card machine. So as long as you don't know my colour code, you won't be able to guess my numbers! Each day of the week has a colour too, mine are not bright but muted, but distinguishable from each other by their general colour shades.

Caroline writes positively about her condition and how it helps her creatively. As a novelist she finds it assists and sparks off ideas for her writing. However, she also says if ideas come too thick and fast it can also create an inertia and gives her writer's block for a while, because she cannot decide which way to go and gets 'petrified by information overload'. Synaethesia has been found to be eight times more common among artists and novelists.

Caroline also poses a question about how her gift sometimes affects her perception of the world. A friend once asked her if she liked her new dress, to which Caroline replied, 'Oh yes, red really suits you,' to which her friend answered 'But the dress is black!'

Caroline's comment on her own perception of this was that she always saw this friend as a 'red' person, so this perception had overridden the blackness of the dress.

From my perspective the condition does not dominate in that way, and I can be more neutral at times. I don't think I would see a black dress as red, but sometimes with another colour tinge to it, such as blue or yellow.

I believe my mother had this condition to some degree and no doubt, as research suggests, I have inherited it from her.

Now, think reader, think about yourself and reflect, could this be your gift too?

***

INSTOW BEACH

As it was a fine day I decided to go to Instow to find out exactly where the Community Chapel, now the venue for the Writing Class, was situated.

The bus ride from Ilfracombe was most pleasant with the sun coming through the windows, first on one side, and then the other as the bus turned in different directions.

I had brought some lunch with me to eat on the beach, but before that, when the bus reached Instow, I stopped to have a cup of coffee at the Wayfarers Inn, not far from Marine Parade. Here, with my drink, I sat at a little table near the front window where I could just glimpse the blue of the sea towards Bideford Bay. As I drank my coffee I read a copy of the *Western Morning News* left for patrons on a shelf near the door. First about the discontent of dairy farmers in the region not receiving a fair deal for the price of their milk and then a report on current political issues and several other short items.

By now it was lunchtime. I left the Inn and walked past the rows of seats that overlook the beach. Many were occupied. Some people looked settled for a while in the sun, others essentially on the move just stopping to eat sandwiches before putting on their backpacks again and moving on. Some perhaps were contemplating an ice cream or a cup of tea.

Maybe for most of us, in some way, the openness and stark elemental nature of the seashore brings out a feeling of not quite knowing what to do. In this ever-growing material and technological age, here we are away from our known world. Some seek the seashore for its simplicity and peace, others may not feel so comfortable with it, but whoever we are, the sea, even at a distance, seems to draw and fascinate us.

I always feel a sense of adventure on a beach, it exposes us in someway. I think, for me, this stems from childhood. When I was a small child, the beach and sea beyond seemed so vast, it was indeed another place. There was always quite a thrill in preparing for it, packing food and towels and bucket and spade for this adventure, as if we were not quite sure what we would have to face.

I walked as far as the Tea Hut then turned in onto the path to the beach. I immediately felt the crunch of golden sand beneath my feet and I flattened them against it in a slightly waddling gait as I walked over the shifting surface.

Here it is interesting how we choose our place, as if setting up a temporary camp – not too near others but where we feel fairly comfortable. I looked around and found a warm, dry spot not far from where some beached boats were upended against the sea wall and two little girls were sitting in the bottom of one each giggling at each other now and then.

I took off my shoes. I ate my sandwich and looked around. On my left, near the block of white flats towards the end of the main beach which rather resembled a moored ship, were two ladies in deck chairs facing the sun. Their chairs were turned slightly towards each other and they chatted continuously. They reminded me of passengers on the deck of a cruise ship with the white flats forming part of the ship itself.

In front, nearer the sea, was a small family. The grandfather, in a navy pullover, had a small black dog on a lead. He stood about while his wife and daughter busied themselves setting out mats and rugs. A little girl looked on and tried to help now and then. The ladies settled themselves and the little girl played. Grandfather stood awkwardly for a while then decided to take the dog for a walk. Maybe he was hesitant about sitting down in case it was difficult to get up again. However, when he came back, with the support of some coats and other items, he did eventually make it, perhaps with the assurances that the others would help him up again if needed.

The tide was half in and there were boats in the bay. By a beached boat two local-looking men were talking and several couples in sunglasses and hats strolled by. Others, further away, resembled pin-like figures as in a Lowry painting going to and fro. In the distance, over the water, Appledore looked fresh against the blue sky and in various spots on the beach children played in the sand.

I looked at my watch. I didn't want to leave it too long to my return journey and about one-thirty I packed up my things and left the beach, made my way along Marine Parade to look for a lane which would lead me up to the main road to find the hall. The lane I found led me up to a bridge over the Tarka Trail and up onto the road. I turned left and walked towards where I thought the hall could be. I eventually found it and went through the gate into the pleasant garden. The door of the hall was open and I could hear voices. A lady was giving some instructions to what sounded like a group of children and I surmised they were a holiday group of some kind. There were several cars in the car park. I stayed a moment or two and admired the view, then made my way back the way I came.

As I walked back, not far along, I came to the top of Quay Lane, the lane where further down is the Village Hall where our previous classes were held. I turned down the lane and was soon back on Marine Parade.

It was a hot day as I waited for my bus to Ilfracombe, and I stood in the shade of a van parked by the quayside not far from the bus stop. Then, because the van owner returned and began to drive it away just as my bus came along, I almost missed it. Fortunately the driver saw me and kindly stopped. Then we were on our way.

It had been a good day. A real seaside day – the first I had had this summer.

***

THE COUNTRY BUS

It was a cold February morning and the first Friday I had come to Barnstaple since before Christmas. I had taken advantage of a fairly dry and much calmer day after several weeks of ominous and continuously fierce and stormy winds and rain.

But it still wasn't a day to stay around too long and, after I had been to the bank, then made a few purchases, first from the Pannier Market where I try to support stallholders with small holdings who grow their own produce, often organically, make cheese and produce yoghurt, and no doubt just about make ends meet. Then into a few specific shops and, after a cup of tea, I made my way, late morning, back to the bus stop to go home.

I had a choice of two routes back to Ilfracombe. The 21 bus along the main road or the 301, known to some as the 'country bus'. The latter wends its way through Muddiford and Bittadon, past woods, a few houses and fields, until it emerges on the crest of a hill. From here, which was once part of Mullacott Moor, there is a spectacular view of the Bristol Channel. You can see Exmoor to the East, Lundy Island to the West, and straight ahead the Welsh coast from the Worm's Head almost up as far as Cardiff.

The place dwarfs the hills, high in themselves, that surround the town, our destination, below. In comparison they seem low and tiny beneath us. Then begins the descent as if on a large, gently bumpy children's slide, slightly exhilarating, with a 'hanging on the edge' feeling and then down and down we go until, almost with a sense of relief, the bus finally draws up in the level High Street in the middle of the town.

So which bus to get today? Well, I thought, the one that comes first in order to get out of the cold and, within a few minutes, the 301 came along.

There were two ladies already on it when three more of us, all of a similar age and carrying shopping, got on. So there were five of us altogether spaced around the single-decker bus. Then a tall, thin man hurried through the door at the last moment, just as the bus was about to leave. I had noticed him briefly as I got on the bus talking animatedly to a lady in the bus shelter and I had heard him say, 'I don't mind which bus it is as long as it gets me there.'

I noticed he had a long black bag with him which turned out to be a guitar case. As he bought his ticket he asked the driver to let him know, 'when we are there,' and added, 'I'm not being funny.'

There was something about him which presented uncertainty and a sense of feeling from the other passengers of wondering where he was going to sit, hoping it would not be with them. Then he came and sat in the empty seat on the opposite side of the aisle to me and I knew, I just knew, he was going to talk to me.

Everyone else looked straight ahead and the lady in front of him, slightly glanced back, more with her eyes than her head, and quickly turned to the front again. I thought to myself if he did speak I would be polite but not get too involved.

As the bus drew away he looked over to me and slightly leaned forward and said, 'I've not had a very good night. I had a brush with the law, and the law won!' I muttered something empathetic. He looked about in his late forties. He was slender with thin dark hair and a slightly undernourished look. There was something almost childlike about him. He was gangly and his blue eyes seemed to be wide open. He had propped his guitar against the seat next to him and I didn't like to look too much in his direction.

I was taking in the view outside when he called over to me and held out an open bag of sweets, 'Have a pineapple chunk.' I looked into the bag of inch cubed squares of luminous yellow and, for some reason, thought of the radioactivity sign, so I smiled and politely declined but thanked him for his offer.

I felt I should not ignore him, that he was someone who tried to be friendly but sometimes didn't quite get it right and was often rebuffed. So we had an occasional short conversation all the way home. At one point he began to sing Country and Western type songs. I imagined he played his guitar, an electric one, and sang in pubs or other places from time to time and may have had an altercation somewhere last night.

He told me later about being in a pub that morning and looking through his TV magazine he'd just bought. He'd pointed out to a man next to him that there was a good comedy film on late in the day. He said the man replied he never watched TV, he listened to the radio instead, the news was better there and he was also quite happy doing the *Daily Mail* crossword. 'Don't some people think they're superior to you reading highbrow newspapers?' he said to me. 'I don't like that; we're all as good as one another.'

I'd initially thought he was going to Ilfracombe for the first time - but now realised he knew some of the shops. He said he felt the numbers were declining. This prompted him into reminiscing about his childhood and going shopping with his mother when they lived in North London. 'Where there were then lots of different shops.'

At one point, as we drove under trees that over arched the road, he remarked, 'It's like being on the London underground.' My guess was he had not been in this area for too long and had not travelled on this route before.

After a pause, he opened a white plastic carrier bag and pulled out a small packet of Parmesan cheese and a jar of tomato sauce declaring, 'These are good for you, you know,' and told me how he was going to cook himself a meal when he got home. I replied it was a good thing to do.

We had only picked up one more passenger on our journey home and in all that time no-one else had looked in his direction, only steadfastly ahead or out of the windows, except for the lady in front of him who had looked rather worried when he began to sing as if he might suddenly lean forward and encourage her to join in.

As we were nearing the end of the journey, he said he hoped he hadn't been a nuisance or talked too much. I replied he hadn't and it had been fine.

When the bus stopped in the High Street and most of us got up to get off, he gathered up his guitar and bag and said to me as he left, 'You see, I had a bad night!'

As I walked away from the bus and along the road towards home, I thought, in a way, I had quite enjoyed my unexpected journey. I was glad I had talked with him. My guess was he was rather a lonely man. Whatever his history, and like many of us from time to time, maybe he had valued some acknowledgment by another person and the acceptance of who he was.

***

APRIL

April cometh – with thy sweetness and sharpness.

On this fine day she bends her delicate lucent face towards me. She touches my cheek as a sweet mother bends over her sleeping child who then awakes to a dear face, a bob of bouncing curls and smiling eyes.

'Come,' she says 'and see the day turn towards the growing light and see what I have brought for thee.'

'What do I see?' The rising angle of the sun marks glazed evergreens with spots of painted light.

Unobtrusive snowdrops, our hope in winter darkness, have slipped away and in their place another, modest, growing silent, softly pale to bright array.

Thin fingers of the trees let the luminescence trickle through to stirring ground and dormant buds, which clung the winter through, sigh, relax and tentatively expand.

Soon the trees thickening with leaves will hide the wood in green. This darkening to become, who can say, maybe a blessing, in the heat of Summer's day.

But then a little chill I feel and draw my coat around as bands of blending clouds, the colour of ice and rain, hover over the widening skies and whip the sun away.

Then did I dream this warmth? Oh, fickle, teasing smile, that offers treasures bright then quickly changes sway.

'Oh, April, you can be the cruellest month,' some say.

It rains – it blows then spasms sun. I am busy keeping warm and watch the sky for hint of change.

Then patterns come, cloud mornings before afternoon blue skies – but chill remains.

Then gradually, aware of lengthening days, I am thankful now for light that we can see, so we can venture outside still, just after tea.

And almost so like that sweet face I soon became aware of all I did not notice, in my haste to welcome Springtime fair.

So quietly given, they have come, the groups of yellow primrose once again to lift the heart and say 'All will be well.'

Then a gradual scatter of bright chrome celandines over the growing grass, and hedgerows offer spots of small white rosettes of blackthorn flowers and beaming golden gorse.

In gardens too, camellias bud and burst in grateful hue, and magnolia cups offer early insects such sweet-loving dew.

And even now forsythia flowers echo yellow too.

We creatures too burst forth, the seagulls have come inland to seek a nest and call and cry, and there is a cockerel I hear at dawn and noon, nearby.

And people touched by the light have come out into the sun and sit in shelters where they meet and talk and then they walk and say, 'Oh Spring has come, oh what a lovely day.'

And April what have I now to say of thee, and thou to me?

'Your hope I love and feel you true and constant I will be to you.'

Then said she to me, 'Oh, forgive me for I am not fully made. I falter too. I pave the way for other lovely things to make parade. To thee I promise you I will be true. Oh, look, look, awake and see what good gifts I really have to offer thee.'

In acknowledgment of William Shakespeare's 400th Birthday. April 2016

***

ALL THE FLOWERS IN MY GARDEN

All the flowers in my garden are gone now – except for the surprise of one small yellow rose. Late it came in the chilly weather after the others had long faded.

It came unexpectedly on the dainty little bush whose flowers usually wave goodbye as summer fades and autumn comes.

But here it was, at first a bud quietly forming, well hidden among the leaves until one day, fading from green to ripe melon, it expanded into the smiling face of a rose no wider than half the length of my thumb. Its neat mandala of pointed petals edging the delicate fruitful tiny stamens.

I felt it looked at me and smiled as if to say 'Well, here I am'. I could see it from my window where it stood out among the green and I talked to it in the garden.

It stayed a while and it cheered me up until it too, satisfied with the gift it had given, sighed and waved goodbye.

Its memory lingers still as the days shorten into longer nights. It had seemed so special to me as if to say to all of us today in the rhythm and routine of daily living, 'Look out for the unexpected joy'.

***

Anne Smith

I'm Anne Smith. I was born, raised and married in Edinburgh, then brought up my two sons in Surrey, before moving to Devon twenty four years ago.

Writing has always been a joy to me, whether composing essays at school; preparing professional reports; or now as part of a group that writes for pleasure. My inspiration is kindled when I walk my dogs along the River Torridge, and is fired by nature's ever changing landscape and the wildlife I see. The human characters in my writings are often based on people I have met or observed in my personal or professional life. Mostly there is a hint of truth in all my stories, but they also provide an outlet for my imagination.

To date I have not published anything. This anthology is my first experience of seeing my name in print. There are more projects in the pipeline. Watch this space!

Anne joined the writing group in 2014 when the classes were held in Bideford. She moved with the group to Instow Village Hall and later to All Saints Chapel. Anne was enthusiastically involved in the production of this anthology, playing a large role in proof-reading and finalising the contributions. Her writing encompassed many styles, humorous stories, descriptive travelogues and enchanting poems. Sadly Anne lost her long battle with cancer shortly before the publication of both this anthology and her own short story for children. As a group we will miss Anne's quiet charm and wit.

A MOMENTARY LAPSE IN REASON

It was only a couple of hours until Ray would be home. She supposed she should think about getting ready. He would take a quick shower then whisk her off to the understated Italian restaurant they both favoured for a special meal. Today was their thirtieth wedding anniversary. Ray had already given her a soppy card; and a beautiful bouquet of red roses had been delivered that morning. But Eleanor had something much more important pressing on her mind. And she wasn't quite sure how she was going to tell Ray about it.

Sitting on the edge of the king size bed, crushing the quilted satin cover, she thought back to when she and Ray had met. She had been twenty two, he had been twenty four. When she saw him in the bar, she was instantly attracted to him. He was tall and slim, dark, with an easy charm. They exchanged a few words. One thing had led to another, and having known each other for only two months, Ray proposed. In her first momentary lapse in reason, Eleanor accepted.

The next day she popped in to see her parents and to tell them her news. Her mother was in the kitchen, baking a Victoria Sandwich for the Coffee and Cake drop in at the local hall the next day. Eleanor sat down on a kitchen stool at the breakfast bar and watched her mother.

1 oz, 2 oz, Eleanor's mother weighed out the flour.

'Mum, do you remember Ray, I brought him round to meet you a couple of weeks ago. Well, he's proposed. We're going to be married.'

3 oz, 4 oz. 'What did you say dear? What are you going to be doing?'

Eleanor repeated herself. Her mother's scream brought her father running from the living room where he had been watching television.

'What's up, what's going on?' he asked in a bewildered tone. He didn't like surprises. He liked calm and normal.

'Eleanor's going to make us a nice cup of tea, then we'll have a little chat,' said her mother.

They had married six weeks later, obviously despite many expressions of doubt and fear. They had cared not for others' opinions. And the marriage had lasted. But now, would it stand the test? Eleanor shook herself, she really ought to be getting ready.

Ray had proved himself to be a committed husband and father. They had two sons, both grown up and living away from home now. Matt had gone to university and was working as something in IT. Luke had rejected university but had studied leisure and travel at college and was a happy travel agent, working hard and seeing a lot of the world as a result. Although different characters, they both seemed to have turned out well. Eleanor was quite happy to take the credit for this.

A large detached house and expensive cars had come at a cost. Ray worked in oil, and logistics, which, in ordinary terms, meant he was responsible for ensuring supplies and deliveries were managed effectively. He travelled extensively in the Far and Middle East and Africa, leaving Eleanor for significant periods of time to juggle her job, the home and their family. After a while, Eleanor found she rather liked it when he was away. She and the boys developed a close bond and shared a relaxed existence together uninterrupted by Ray's presence. In some indefinable way, when Ray returned, normal routines crumpled to accommodate Ray's needs. Or thinking about it, his demands.

No doubt, some of it was down to Ray's personality. As he had aged, matured, gained success, he had grown more opinionated. He seemed to have lost his sense of humour. She was tired of his charm. He was full of his own importance. And he always had to be right. This had led to arguments with the boys. Ray expected their respect but, as young intelligent adults, he rarely considered theirs. He was always ready with a put down if it would satisfy his need for supremacy. Eleanor tried gently to guide Ray into a more equal relationship with his sons, but although he listened, he was unable to change. Gradually, the boys accepted their father as he was and of course now were leading their own very different lives.

Eleanor too had taken the path of least resistance, acknowledging Ray's good points and ignoring his less attractive traits. Eleanor had been born with an inbuilt tolerance and acceptance of people and their ways. In contrast to Ray, she'd had little direct experience of different races and cultures, but she tended to think the best of people. Ray was very patronising towards others, be they of a different colour or a different creed. When Eleanor challenged him, his trump card was always that he had worked with 'these people' and knew what they were like. Eleanor admitted she didn't know 'these people' but imagined they had the same hopes and aspirations as she had. Ray generalised: blacks were lazy, black people with power were corrupt, Chinese were cunning, migrants were after an easy life. His mind inhabited the days of the Raj, of white man supremacy, when native people were kept in their inferior place. There had been a horrible situation recently when Matt started going out with an Indian girl. Eleanor had found her charming and interesting, but Ray had spurned her, purely on the grounds of her colour. The situation was finally resolved, but not without breaking Matt's heart, when the girl's parents insisted that she had a traditional Indian marriage and stopped her from seeing Matt. And that was when enough became enough. For the second time in her life, Eleanor had a momentary lapse in reason.

It was incredible what one could find out on the internet these days. Eleanor had spent hours researching, and googling companies, then following up leads with email enquiries. She had downloaded the necessary initial paperwork and submitted the relevant applications. With Ray away again on business, she had carried it out in secrecy, even managing a trip away to complete the final paperwork and shop for a few necessary items of clothing. She had bought reference books and hidden them under the bed. And now everything was completed as far as it could be, and she was ready. Except she hadn't yet told Ray of her intention.

The slamming of the front door broke into her daydream and Eleanor realised that she hadn't even begun to get ready for dinner. She heard Ray put down his brief case in the hall, and go into the kitchen. He would see the roses on the central island where she had placed them for maximum effect. At this time of evening the light from the westward facing window would catch them in the sun's rays. She heard the clink of glasses and imagined that he had found the bottle of chilled champagne in the fridge. Still she sat on the bed. She heard Ray's footsteps on the stairs and then, there he was, taking up space in the bedroom doorway. And there she was, unshowered, in jeans and a tee shirt.

Ray's expression was quizzical, with maybe a hint of annoyance. After all he had given her a card, sent flowers, booked a table at their favourite restaurant and rushed home early from work.

'Hi,' Eleanor's voice hesitated. She had nothing now to lose. It was as well he knew. She would only be uncomfortable during the meal if she stalled.

Reaching under the bed, she pulled out a clear plastic envelope with her paperwork inside, and the Lonely Planet's Guide to India.

'I'm going to India, soon, for two months. I'm going to be on a project with young Indian women, helping to empower them. I shall be living and working with them.' She'd almost said with 'those people'. Avoiding Ray's face, she kept her eyes cast downwards. The tension was unbearable. She waited for Ray's outburst and his patronising comments. She wished the ground would open and swallow her up. Finally, Ray broke the chasm of silence.

'Well, that is something to celebrate. Let's go downstairs and grab a glass of champagne and you can tell me all about it.'

REFLECTIONS

Football players overpaid.
Football matches underplayed.
Moguls with money to blow.
Not on local talent though.
That's what gets my goat.

X Factor wannabe stars.
Dazzling bling and flashy cars.
All with fur and no knickers.
Jumped up nobs, city slickers.
That's what gets my goat.

Kids at risk, stranger danger,
World Wide Web and civil war.
Lies, threats and exploitation,
Shame, fear and mutilation.
That's what gets my goat.

All lives follow nature's path
Kind or cruel, fair or harsh.
Would humans be the players
To act as loving carers.

To give, not take, to count costs
to others; no greed, no lust,
Tolerance, compassion just.
That would float my boat!

Anne Smith

JACK AND BILLY

It was one of those days which couldn't decide what it was going to do. Blue sky was interspersed with dark clouds, which, since the early hours of the morning, had dropped rain showers over the countryside. Now the sun was shining; raindrops were sparkling on the grass and dropping off the branches of the trees at the edge of the field. Jack walked round his field, occasionally stopping to chew on some grass; waiting for his working day to begin.

Beyond the field, further up the rough track, Billy was getting ready too. He had been up since first light, and was dressed and breakfasted ready for the coming working day. Would the sun continue to shine, or was the rain going to dominate the day? Billy opted to wear a tweed jacket just in case the latter was the case. He put it on over a blue check shirt and yellow neckerchief. He'd already pulled on his strong leather boots and tucked in his woollen trousers. Leaving the house behind, he set off down the track to find Jack.

Billy was eighteen years of age and had been Jack's worker for two years. He had walked the canal since he'd left school at fourteen. He hadn't excelled at school and was happy to leave as soon as he could. He much preferred being outdoors and his job with Jack suited him well.

Jack spied Billy walking down the track and trotted up to the gate to meet him. This had become a daily ritual and both enjoyed their first greetings of the day. Jack snorted at Billy, who stroked Jack's head, and spoke gently to him, telling him they would have a good day together.

Billy put Jack's head collar on and led him out to the barn to fit his harness. Together, the two made their way down the track, across the meadow, over the ditch towards the canal, where Jack would pull a tug boat full of lime, which would be distributed between the tenant farmers to spread over their fields to increase crop yield. They joined a team of five more men and horses who would form the caravan travelling the distance to the last lime kiln, some twelve miles upriver.

Jack and Billy were the last in the line. Billy liked it this way as he could drop back and put some distance between himself and the next man, making the most of what solitude he could have. For most of the way, the canal followed a similar path to the river. It was higher than the river, often twenty feet above the flowing waters. Billy loved walking the towpath, with Jack alongside him, and being able to see the expansive landscape, the animals, the birds, the insects and the plants that thrived along the banks. The early snowdrops had disappeared, as had the pungent wild garlic. Now, in early summer, he could smell the heady honeysuckle, intertwining with blackberry tendrils and prickly wild rose. Vivid blue damsel flies flitted above him and birds chattered in the trees.

The ambivalent early morning weather had evolved into a warm, dry day. The sun was shining, drying up the last of the raindrops. Billy and Jack were walking quietly, Billy thinking thoughts of nothing much. His attention was suddenly taken by something glinting in a tree down by the river. Telling Jack to 'whoa, boy' (he knew Jack would wait for him, and Jack, being strong and fit, would soon catch up with the others) half running, half sliding he went to investigate. Hanging from a small branch he found a necklace. It was a cameo of the head of a woman, encircled with tiny diamond like stones and set in silver. It was a beautiful piece of jewellery. Billy pondered a few minutes, wondering what to do with it. Someone must be missing it but who? There was no-one around. A whinny from Jack roused him. He pocketed the necklace and continued along the towpath with Jack.

Returning to the same spot later that afternoon, Billy saw a young girl, a bit younger than himself, seemingly searching for something and Billy's hand went to the pocket where he had put the necklace. He made his way down the slope towards the girl. He didn't recognise her; she wasn't from the village; even her dress was unfamiliar to him. She wore thick, blue trousers, a white cotton blouse, and soft shoes rather than the stout leather boots generally worn. Much less modest than the clothes the local girls wore.

In reply to his question, she told him she had been at this spot the previous day with friends. They'd had a picnic and a swim in the river, and it was not until she was home that she missed her necklace. Billy wondered where home was. He made a pretence of looking for it and asked her what it looked like. She described the necklace he had found earlier. Taking it from his pocket, he held it out towards her. Her joy at being reunited with it was obvious, and she explained that it had belonged to her great grandmother; that her great grandmother had lived around here and had married a local boy who, like him, had worked the canal. But when the railways came, the canal was closed, he lost his job and went to work on merchant ships. He had brought the necklace back from Ceylon. Billy had never heard of Ceylon, and the girl explained it was near India but that nowadays it was called Sri Lanka.

Confused, Billy excused himself. 'I must get back to Jack', nodding towards Jack, who was waiting patiently for Billy.

'Jack' the girl said, 'my grandfather was called Jack and it's been a family joke that he was called after a horse'.

Billy was thoughtful on the way home, uncertain as to what he had just experienced. There was to be a dance at the village hall this coming Saturday. Perhaps he would go. He might meet the girl again, or perhaps the girl of his dreams.

***

ICE HOTEL

Ice stored
Ice carved
Ice honed
Ice hotel

Artists assigned
Hotel designed
Rooms to decorate
With themes elaborate.
Creating reality
From spirituality.

Temperatures low
Chambers of snow
Who will lie low
In rooms aglow
With electricity
And eccentricity?

Bar chilled
Glasses filled
Liquor veined
Drinks drained
Thirst sated
Headiness gained

Chapel lighting
Subtle, inviting
Atmospheres amazing
For weddings
And christenings
And contemplatings

Ice stored
Ice carved
Sun shone
Hotel gone.

MAURICE AND MARJORIE

Maurice poured out three cups of tea from the silver teapot and smiled thinly across the table at his guests. They had been friends of Marjorie's, and with other neighbours and ex-colleagues had rallied together to sympathise and support Maurice following the dreadful accident.

Maurice replaced the teapot on the hot mat. He was a traditionalist and liked to maintain standards. He and Marjorie had always had afternoon tea out of the silver tea pot. It had been his mother's originally, and he hadn't paid it much attention until Marjorie took a bit of a shine to it. So when his mother died, they had kept it.

Maurice snapped out of his daydream and responded politely to his guests' questions and observations, while secretly wishing they would leave. Leave him in peace and quiet.

Peace and quiet. They had moved into their bungalow three years ago when they had both retired. Maurice had been a school teacher, a profession he admired but felt totally uncomfortable with. He had no sense of connection with the children and young people at the school, and they had felt no connection with him. He was not one of the most popular teachers and there had been no tears shed when he left. Marjorie on the other hand, had been a popular member of the team at work, where she was a medical receptionist. Her gentle voice, her empathy and kindness had won her affection and respect from doctors, colleagues and patients alike.

The bungalow stood on its own, inside a pretty garden. A gate led to a path which meandered its way to a little cove, which they could see from the bay window in the lounge. It really was idyllic. And although it was not a private beach, so few people ever found their way to it, that it felt as though it was theirs and theirs alone. Peace and quiet.

On that fateful day, after tea, Marjorie had suggested they went for a walk down to the cove. There was a bit of a wind blowing in from the sea, but it was sunny and quite pleasant. They strolled along the sand, Marjorie picking up shells as she went, loving their subtle colours. Maurice strode ahead, ignoring the beauty surrounding him. He could hear Marjorie talking to him, and ignored her too. Chuntering, Marjorie was always chuntering. What she found to talk about, he really didn't know. Who was interested in the minutiae she managed to regurgitate over and over again? It had always been so. When they had first met he thought she bubbled like a clear, sparkling brook down a hillside. She had been attracted to him by his quiet calm and steadiness. But since they'd retired, he had become increasingly annoyed by her incessant chattering. It drove him mad; disturbed his peace and quiet. And what was worse, Marjorie was usually up first and then he had to share his breakfast with blooming Chris Evans, and afternoon tea with Steve what's-his-name and his insignificant guest celebrities.

Their walk had taken them towards some rocks, which they had to cross to reach the sand on the other side of the cove. Maurice was ahead, Marjorie behind him, still chattering. The rocks were slippery and they needed to take care. Maurice turned round towards Marjorie who was in mid-leap between rocks. Even to himself, he would always claim it was unpremeditated. He stuck out his right foot, catching Marjorie's booted leg just above the ankle. She fell heavily, hitting her head against a rock. Maurice stood stock still for several minutes. Marjorie didn't move. The tide had turned some hours ago. If he didn't get help quickly, she would be swallowed up by the surging waters and would drown.

Maurice walked away, back up the path to the bungalow. He sat down in the chair in the bay window and consulted his book of Tide Times. From time to time he examined the beach through his binoculars. Just before dusk, he returned to the cove. The tide had turned again. For the second time in a few hours he made his way back up the path to the bungalow. Once inside, he dialled 101 and reported his wife missing. The Police questioned Maurice who expressed his distress calmly and quietly. He explained that Marjorie had gone for a walk on the beach. He had fallen asleep in his chair and had only wakened up when darkness was gathering. The policeman was sympathetic and asked no further questions. The police alerted the coastguards. Marjorie's body was found three days later, washed ashore in another cove some miles away. The coroner recorded her death as accidental.

It was a small funeral. They hadn't had children, intimacy not featuring strongly in their relationship. Their parents were dead and Marjorie's elder sister was too ill to travel. A few ex-colleagues and neighbours attended the simple service and promised to keep in touch with Maurice. Which they did, but most of the time, Maurice enjoyed his own company, in peace and quiet.

***

SWEDISH LAPLAND – A WINTER WONDERLAND

We walked tentatively along the board walk, keeping to the rugs laid down to give our feet protection, then opened the door to the sauna, went in, quickly shutting it behind us, keen to keep the heat in and the cold out. The sauna had been lit two hours ago and was now up to temperature. It was a traditional sauna, fired by wood, its smell pleasantly filling the room. Someone threw on more water; the stones sent steamy heat up to the top bench. The feeling of total warmth was a comfort.

That morning we had left the hotel and driven along icy roads through endless pine and fir forest before reaching our destination. Annette welcomed us warmly, but made sure we stayed up in the reception area until Andreas said he was ready.

We were, we hoped, suitably dressed. Two base layers, a fleece and jogging bottoms, overalls; two pairs of socks and double skin boots, two pairs of gloves, balaclava and fur hat. That should do.

The noise increased as the huskies were prepared. Thirty dogs, tethered together in sixes behind five sleds. Thirty dogs were howling, yowling, barking, larking around, sitting and leaping. 'Let's go, let's go, I want to go now!'

Andreas and the dogs were ready and after a short briefing we took our places in two's on the sleds, one sitting, one driving. Ready, steady, with howls of anticipation and excitement we were off, pulled along behind twenty four, red socked paws, working in unison, man and dogs, together a team.

We drove along the frozen lake. It was eleven in the morning. The sun was tipping the tops of the trees, and was fully up. Its orange ball dominated the southern sky, but the shadows were long, stretching fifty metres or so over the ice and snow. The sky was a cloudless blue. The snow was alight with millions and millions of tiny, sparkling diamonds. At times, depending on the light and shade, the ground shone blue, a clear icy hue creating a magical winter wonderland.

The dogs had calmed now. They were over their initial excitement, but still wanted to run and run, and to overtake the ones in front given half a chance. We were the last sled, and we watched the snaking line traverse the lake, skirting the pine and fir forest, its trees enshawled in wraps of snow, boughs bent low by the weight, or merely dipped in deference to nature in winter. The ground was swathed in clouds of warm dog breath.

Sitting on the sled had been cold, so cold. It was 22 degrees centigrade. We had quickly adopted the local habit of dropping the superfluous minus. But now, driving the sled, there was much to do: watching ahead, using the metal foot plate to slowly and gently brake the dogs, whenever they came too close to the sled in front, leaning to turn the sled, steering the dogs, keeping them in the track.

Cold hands, cold feet, eyelashes stuck together with ice, icicles on moustaches, hair icily frizzed, balaclavas damp and frozen by our own breath. Cameras frozen, mobile phones frozen, goggles iced over. Technology struggling, humans just coping, dogs enjoying.

After two hours we returned to the kennels to be greeted with barks and howls from the twenty huskies left behind today. It would be their turn tomorrow. We fed the dogs treats of frozen salmon cake, and gave them hugs. For us, there was hot Lindonberry juice, hot vegetable soup, cooked in a cauldron over a wood fire lit in the tepee. Good, but we were shivering and couldn't stop.

Now, back at the hotel, the heat in the sauna soothed our bodies, creating a sense of wellbeing and comfort. Soon it would be time for dinner in the cosy, candlelit dining room of the hotel.

Then later, with a glass of wine, and dinner just served, the call went up.

'The Northern Lights are coming.'

Knives and forks clattered, plates of food were abandoned. We rushed to the boot room to clobber up into our warm clothing. We walked out onto the lake, lay down on a reindeer skin in the snow, and watched the show begin.

Cold, oh yes, thirty degrees of cold. But it was only cold. And God it was good. No words can describe how good.

***

THE DILEMMA

Sam had just wakened. In the gap between the curtains, on the other side of the window, he could see it wasn't quite dawn yet, but that the moon, which had been full last night, was sharing its cool silver light with the chilly November morn. A predatory light thought Sam. The foxes would be hunting, taking advantage of the misty cover. The barn owl would be out on the wing, searching for a tasty morsel, a vole or a mouse, still too sheathed in sleep to be alert to the danger approaching silently from above.

Sam stretched out his long, well toned body. He flexed his muscular limbs, in a masculine sort of way, and then relaxed. He was lying in the curve of Helen's back. Tentatively, he nestled closer, reaching out to her, appreciating the comfort of her body. She made no physical movement, no tangible response, but he sensed withdrawal, rejection. Experience had told him not to push it.

He could see it was getting lighter outside, so Sam rose, and went downstairs. Having sated his thirst and a pang of hunger with a drink of milk, he went outside and studied the surrounding landscape.

The cool glow from the moon had all but gone now, superseded by a warm light dusting of pinks and lilacs from the morning sun rising low and slowly in the east just beyond the Douglas Firs on the other side of the creek. A crowd of white egrets was roosting under the cover of the trees' canopies, their black stick-like legs tucked under their white downy feathers. He could sense rather than actually smell the faint saltiness in the air, blown in from the estuary on the south easterly wind. A fair day would be welcome after the storms of the last few days, when choppy waves had rocked the little boats at anchor off the pier; the strong winds had finally laid bare the trees, even the beech trees; their empty boughs now captured in silhouette against the sun.

He stepped through the fallen leaves in the garden, reaching the top of the lane which led to the creek. The ground was soft and damp underfoot. The dying bracken, in brilliant autumnal hues, had been flattened but still afforded good ground cover for little mammals. When he was younger, he might have gone off prepared to bag a rabbit or two, but now he was content to leave those sorts of pursuits to others.

He lingered for a while, not for any particular reason, but because he was in no hurry. He watched a fisherman on the pier, ritualistically laying out his paraphernalia – rod, reel, bucket, and bait; preparing to go on board, hoping to catch his breakfast. The thought of breakfast awoke Sam's taste buds and alerted him to an empty stomach. He turned back towards home, up the lane, through the gate to the garden and round the side of the house. Surely Helen would be up and about by now. Hopefully, she'd started to think about breakfast.

There were no lights on downstairs, no sign of life. Here was his dilemma. He had to make a decision. Did he go round the back and in through the flap, or should he feign forgetfulness and wake the household. Oh, what the heck. Meioow!

***

Anne Smith

THE PIGEON LOFT

They seemed to have been flying around all weekend. Rushing here, flapping there, from one town to the next. Location, location, location. That's what it was all about. She'd been perfectly happy in Trafalgar Square. There was a regular supply of quality, fresh street food, and their lodgings were comfortable enough, just one room but good thick cardboard, and quite large enough now the family had flown the nest. Her kids and grand kids were close by, Suzie and Richard over in the Aldwych, Eric and Barbara settled at Covent Garden, and the rest of the girls all had places at UCL. They had done very well for themselves.

But oh dear, Billie had got this idea into his head. He wanted to escape to the country for a quieter life in his retirement. And he wanted to go north. Did he have any idea of how cold the north could be? She'd argued her case, but in the end, had relented for the sake of peace. They had gone looking for a place in the country, and were now in Whitby, in Yorkshire.

They'd already dismissed ten possible lodgings – too small, too draughty, too low, too high.

Now they were viewing the eleventh. But even Millie had to admit this one had potential. 'Coo, Coo,' she exclaimed.

'Wow,' said Billie.

At this point they were standing outside The Loft, on the outside decking area. From here there was a good view of the sea.

'I've always wanted a sea view,' sighed Billie.

'Billie, you're a pigeon. You have wings, by default you fly. If you got off your backside, you could see the sea from wherever you live. And besides, it smells of fish and chips.'

It was true; there was a fish and chip shop, directly underneath The Loft, belching smoke from its air vent into the atmosphere.

'Just think of the positives, Ducks: warm, fresh fish for protein; a healthy supply of carbs; and the tomato ketchup is one of your five a day. And, where there's fish and chips, there's ice cream. You couldn't ask for more, not really.' cajoled Billie.

Well, that might be true, but the seagulls would be fighting competition.

'What do you think of the neighbourhood?' asked Billie.

Millie preened and looked around, taking her time before replying. There were rows of terraced houses, very close together, with small gardens. Most of the houses had lofts, and it was quite noisy. It was all a bit higgledy-piggledy, not like the Square with its formal boundaries, and classical buildings. These streets were full of cars, bicycles and buses. The cold easterly wind blew directly towards them. The local guys and dolls looked a bit dowdy. She had to admit, Billie and she made a lovely couple with their speckled wings, fantails and flashes of pearly white down. 'I think I'd miss the space, and the peace and quiet of the Square,' she mused.

They both wandered over, closer to The Loft.

'I like the colour, Billie. It's tasteful, a sort of Farrow and Ball green, don't you think? And it has a look of Art Deco styling.'

'Well, I'm not sure it's what I would choose, but I could live with it.' Billie peered inside. 'Oh, it's got beams. I like its character. It's not just a cardboard box. Someone has taken a lot of care renovating this to a high standard, yet maintaining its original features.'

'So, what do you think, my Millie? Should we wing it and take the plunge?'

'By eck, a' reet,' said Millie, trying out the local vernacular.

Billie hopped inside, followed by Millie. As dusk faded to night, they hunkered down, fluffed up their feathers, and snuggled up together, their necks and heads forming a heart shape, just like the swans they'd seen in hotel bedrooms. So be it. Let Billie have his day. And if she didn't like it here, she could always fly back to the Square!

Anne Smith

THE TREE

Rising from the house that faced the Jarvis Hills in the long distance, there was a tower for the day birds to build in and for the owls to fly around at night. From the village the light in the tower window shone like a glow worm through the panes; but the room under the sparrows' nests was rarely lit; webs were spun over its unwashed ceilings; it stared over twenty miles of the up and down county, and the corners kept their secrets where there were claw marks in the dust.

The child knew the house from roof to cellar; he knew the irregular lawns and the gardener's shed where the flowers burst out of their jars; but he could not find the key that opened the door of the tower.

Dylan Thomas

The child had never been into the tower. His mother forbade it. A loving, kind mother, she was 'she who must be obeyed'. But now idle curiosity had flared up into all-consuming questions. The comings and goings of last night had fed his imagination until he needed answers. Even frightening answers would be better than frightening questions.

The tower was on the dark, northern side of the house, the antithesis of the sunny lawn, which provided the vehicle for his play. Here, there was no lawn mimicking a lake or seashore or sky. Rather, there was a woodland of mystery, darkness and ghostly matters. Dominating all the other trees, mainly leylandii, planted rudely by the people who had lived in the house before the child had been born, was an oak tree, massive and dead. Not a leaf clung to its twigs, not a branch was dressed in green. Its upper limbs spread out like a messiah addressing his flock. Its stature, proclaiming it to have been a fine tree, of some importance to the topography of the area, was now, like an old man, creaking under the strain of standing upright.

Determined, but without a key, the child was impotent. Dropping the bag he carried, he crouched down and peered with a squinting eye through the keyhole. It was a large keyhole, as would be the key if only he could find it. The metal plate around the hole was rusting and no longer shiny black. It matched the hinges, attaching the door to the oak architrave, itself blackened with age. The wooden planks of the door were uneven in width and had separated, only enough to provide further squinting opportunities, not rotten enough for entry to the tower.

From his one-eyed view of the interior of the tower, he could see a flight of uneven stone steps rising in a curve, upwards towards a landing, from where further steps would take an intruder to the top level. Discounting the spiders' webs, suggesting spiders were alive and well in the tower, there was no sign of life. Even the claw marks in the corners signalled the passing of time. No sign of human footsteps disturbed the dust covering the steps. So how to explain the voices he'd heard last night? Had bodies ascended, Harry Potter like on broomsticks, to light the light in the window and talk out loud to disturb a boy's slumber? The child shivered.

The wind, which had been high in the sky, and silent, changed and took on a new swirling energy, blowing the child's hair into his eyes and stirring the trees until their movements resembled waves on the ocean. Dark clouds blasting in front of the sun placed dancing shadows on the ground. The man stood, swaddled inside the leylandii, casting no shadow, obscure, mysterious. He watched the child intently, taking mindful measure of his looks, his uninhibited, unspoken gestures.

The child retrieved his bag, searching its contents for something useful. He had brought an assortment of things from the house. Some were his standard kit – elastic bands, a magnet, wire and twine, a magnifying glass, a packet of crisps. Others had been secretly displaced when no-one was looking; items that wouldn't be missed immediately. He had borrowed the gardener's binoculars, but these were only of use if he could get into the tower. Dare he use his penknife to pick at the lock? The philips screwdriver was useless on the domed nuts attaching the hinges. Something, guilt probably, made him shiver again and he turned, looking around him. The wind still blew, evoking inhuman sounds from the trees, which were now bending and swaying to some classical symphony, except the oak tree, which stood sentinel like, as if waiting to conduct a ceremony.

The man, tall and imposing, stepped out from the trees. A man, who walked with confidence in his step, though now he hesitated behind the oak tree's smooth trunk. Again he watched the child. When the child had been born, in his mind he had foreseen this day. He approached closer, a sigh escaped him that must have been louder than he thought, because the child turned round and saw his dark, windproofed figure. The child froze, inflexible as a gravestone, staring and anticipating. 'Father?' Holding out the key towards the child he cried out, 'My son, my child!'

***

MADDY AND THE DUSTBIN MAN

The Button

Here it was again. Friday, so soon. Time, to Maddy, flew past too quickly. She always seemed to be lagging behind the clock. The only thing she wouldn't be late for would be her own funeral, because some-one else would be responsible for getting her there on time. Hurriedly, she went round the house gathering up the rubbish in the waste bins, emptying the kitchen bin and tying the tops of the polythene bags.

She could see the dustcart rounding the corner at the top of her street. She lived lower down the steep hill but it would soon be outside her door. Neatly placed by the other residents at the edge of the pavement, the black wheelie bins, were collected by the dustmen and their contents emptied onto the mashers in the cart. Slowly the dustcart crept along the kerb, coming ever closer to Maddy's house.

She wasn't ready, why did they always have to come on time? Why couldn't they be late, just once?

The November air outside was chilly, and the roads glistened with a smear of dampness. She thrust her feet into the warm, fur lined bootee slippers her daughter had bought her as a birthday present a few weeks ago. Her bare legs peeked on show between the top of the bootees and the hem of her brown skirt. She threw on a cardigan, an oversized cardigan for her petite figure. Too big for Maddy, because it had been Tom's. It was warm and so comfortable, and in much too good condition to give to the local charity shop. Just wearing it brought Tom alive to her again.

Tom had been the organiser, the practical person who held their home together, the person who put out the bins every Friday. And now, inadequate Maddy muddled along, stumbling from one mess towards another disaster.

She couldn't even manage to put out the rubbish on time. She pulled the grey chunky cardigan around her, doing up the single, large, brown, woven leather button. Then she gathered up the four bags of rubbish from the kitchen floor, rushed out of the door, and scuffed down the short path to try to meet the dustcart.

Inside the gate, her wheelie bin waited in anticipation. She grabbed it and attempted to steer it through the gate and onto the pavement, at the same time stuffing the bags into its pungent depths. They wouldn't take the rubbish unless it was inside the wheelie bin and the lid was closed. The dustbin men were relentless in their task. They inched steadily towards her. Almost there. Three bags in and one to go. The dustcart drew up alongside. Panicking, Maddy lunged at the wheelie, pushing the last bag in, and shutting down the lid firmly. There they would take it now.

Except that, in her haste, Maddy had caught her cardigan between the lid and the body of the wheelie. She was held securely, trapped by the large, brown, leather button. Sadly, her lunge to bury the last bag had unsteadied the wheelie. It set off on its own path across the pavement, over and down the kerb. Taken off guard, Maddy held on, pushing down on the wheelie's lid. The wheelie gathered pace and Maddy's legs came off the ground. By now, her hands were firmly clamped round the lid; her cardigan still trapped by its button.

Maddy's journey atop the wheelie took her across the road, in front of the dustcart.

'Hey, missus, we haven't emptied that one yet,' yelled the dustbin man. Unable to think of a smart reply, she yelled back, 'Tough!' and carried on.

On the opposite pavement, Mr Grant's dog, Dennis, was watering the lamppost.

'Good morning, Maddy,' Mr Grant greeted her.

'Morning,' she gasped, her mouth twisting to form the words, as the wheelie headed towards the lamppost, startling Dennis and stopping him in mid-flow.

At this point, had Maddy slid off, she might have saved the day, and some of her dignity. But she decided to try to grab the lamppost. One arm raised ready, she swayed her body towards it. The wheelie, on wet stones, reacted to the sudden movement, spun on its wheels and took off down the hill.

A sudden gust of wind, blowing down the street, whipped up and under the folds of Maddy's skirt, exposing her pale legs and purple M & S knickers. Her skirt filled with air, spinnaker fashion, and the wheelie sailed on ever faster. In despair, she raised both arms into the air.

The dustcart had been making steady progress down the hill.

'Hey, missus, you're on a wheeliebin, not the bloomin' Titanic'. Four fingers appeared above her outstretched arms, silencing the bemused dustman.

By now, a small crowd had gathered to watch, or avoid, Maddy's progress down the hill; and a few cars had stopped; not to mention the approaching double decker bus. The driver swore. He had a timetable to follow and couldn't be late, not even for a runaway wheelie bin with a mad woman on top of it.

Maddy could see the main road ahead, and beyond that the calm waters of the river, flowing predictably towards the estuary. For a brief second, the last few moments replayed in her mind, and she questioned her fate.

But then, the slippery cobbles and the wobbly wheels combined forces, and the wheelie was sent off course again. It turned, sliding sideways down the hill, until it bumped against the steps of the local public house, halting its downward journey towards the river. It fell over, disgorging its contents onto the steps.

Finally, the stress must have proved too much, for the button gave up its struggle to remain attached to the warm, grey, chunky cardigan and popped. Released from her captive state, Maddy had the presence of mind to let go and slid indelicately to her knees in the road. Cross and embarrassed, she stood up, smoothed down her skirt, gathered the cardigan around her, and too shaken to walk up the hill towards home, started up the steps to the pub, abandoning her wheelie bin. The crowd began to disperse. The cars and the bus moved on up the hill.

The dustcart had slowly and meticulously continued moving down the hill.

At the top of the steps, she turned to see the conscientious dustman pick up the rubbish and right the wheelie bin. She sighed, shrugged her shoulders, and turned to go into the pub, where, even at this early hour, a port and lemon beckoned.

'Hey missus, see you next week then,' called the dustbin man.

***

Barbara Ferris

Barbara Ferris was born and brought up in Surrey and over the years has lived in Aylesbury in Buckinghamshire, Thame in Oxfordshire and Whitby, North Yorkshire. She also spent five years in southern Spain. She has always enjoyed writing and, since her retirement, has found time to draw from her experiences in life and put pen to paper. Since joining the writing group she has produced many short stories and has managed to complete her novel which she started in 1991.

FEBRUARY

Marjorie was fed up with being stuck indoors. The weather hadn't been kind these last few weeks. It had either been too wet, too cold, even icy, not nice, or safe, to go for a walk. And Marjorie loved to walk, on her own if possible then she could go at her own pace and not hold anyone up. She couldn't do much else now. After all, she was eighty years old and though her mind wanted to do all sorts of things, her body told her otherwise. But today the sun was shining, the sky was blue with no menacing black clouds and she was determined to get out. If she wrapped up warm in her thick winter coat with her scarf tied snugly round her neck and her hands ensconced in the fur lined gloves her grandson had bought her for Christmas, she was sure she'd be warm enough. She'd take that horrible hat with the bobble on just in case she got cold.

Now, where could she go? Obviously she would have to get the bus, there wasn't anywhere nice to go round where she lived, not on the estate. She knew where she would like to go, but could she manage it? Yes, why not. She'd take her stick and go carefully, and not too far. She just wanted to see the water and smell the countryside. She'd take her mobile phone which her daughter had insisted on buying for her, just in case. She was sure she could work out how to use it if she had to. Oh, and she'd better leave a note to say she'd gone for a walk just in case anyone called in and wondered where she was.

The bus dropped her at the end of the lane. The driver was a bit concerned about leaving her in what looked like the middle of nowhere, but she assured him she would be OK. She knew she had to be back for the return bus at 15 minutes past the hour. She had her watch, so she would be fine.

She walked slowly, picking her way along the path, avoiding the gnarled roots of the trees and treading carefully among the loose stones. She had her stick to steady her as she looked up at the trees, ready to burst into leaf, and breathed in the smell. She closed her eyes and remembered. She'd run and skipped along this path with George and Rod and Josie and all her other friends from school whose names she could not now recall. They would scramble down the bank and paddle in the shallow water of the stream, always cold even in the height of summer. She'd walked this same path, hand in hand, with her sweetheart, later to become her husband. They had brought their children here to run and skip and scramble down the banks just as she had done. It was her favourite place. She walked on, taking her time. Because of all the rain during the last couple of months, the stream was full. She stood and watched as sticks and dead leaves rushed past her. A squirrel dashed up a tree, did he not know it was still winter? She smiled, Spring must be just round the corner. If she continued to the end of the path she would reach the waterfall at Falling Foss where the stream cascaded over the rocks into the river and onwards to the sea. But she didn't have the time or the energy to walk to the waterfall, she would only go a little way. She was glad she'd come alone, she didn't want the distraction of anyone with her while she remembered.

She reached the hermit's cave. As children, they had been afraid to go in, afraid the hermit would chase them. When they were older, they did venture in, still with a little trepidation even though they knew the hermit had been dead for at least 400 years. She smiled again. It seemed so long ago now. She poked her head into the cave – it smelt musty and damp and looked just like any cave she'd ever seen. Why had they been so afraid? She wondered if the modern children ever even bothered to come here. She'd have to bring her grandchildren when they came to visit, they would enjoy it.

She looked around for somewhere to rest. There was a very convenient wooden bench a few yards further on, that hadn't been there the last time she'd come. There was a plaque on the back 'In memory of Arthur Simons who liked to walk this path – 1925-2005.' She sank down onto the seat and rested her legs.

February

'Thank you Arthur Simons, whoever you were.' She spoke quietly, although there was no one to hear her. She sat there for a few minutes, then looked at her watch. It was time to start back for the bus.

She turned round and made her way slowly back along the path to the road. She felt so much better for the walk. The sun was still shining, she was warm and cosy and the bus should be there in about ten minutes. Maybe she would come again soon, when it was a bit warmer. She'd better not tell her daughter where she'd been though, she'd only tell her off for going so far on her own. No, better keep quiet.

***

Barbara Ferris

THE CLEAROUT

I thought I'd clean the cupboards out
Start the New Year right
Sort out all the contents,
Clear out all the rubbish, put it out of sight

I started in the kitchen, took out everything
Tins of beans, a tin of rice and a tin of pears
I should have used them months ago
But I'd forgotten they were there.

I found a pack of soya custard,
I'm not very keen
I could give it to the food bank
But the date is March thirteen.

There's that balsamic vinegar
I bought when I lived in Spain
It looks all right, it smells OK
It's only 8 years old, I'll put it back again

The next thing that I tackled
Was the drawer with odds and ends
A metal box held batteries and matches,
Screws and nails and defunct pens.

The Clearout

There's cocktail sticks and roasting sticks
They'll be useful I am sure
I think I'd better keep them,
Don't want to have to buy some more.

There's a painted metal soldier
And a plastic thing with legs
All tangled up with garden string
And several useful looking pegs

That lethal tube of superglue
I can't throw that away
Though every time I use it
My fingers stick for days

Then there are the teacloths, I'll fold them up all neat
There's one my grandson gave me, there's his little face
His class made it in primary school
Dated nineteen ninety eight.

I don't know what is useful,
I don't know what is not
But when they come to clear it out when I am here no more
The last thing they will think about is my untidy drawer,

They'll look at it and wonder why I kept these things
The screws and pegs and batteries, all in the little tin.
They'll pick it up and tip it out
Straight into the bin.

MEMORIES

I have so many memories of when I was young, it seems so long ago now. Some of my most precious memories are of my grandmother. I always thought I was lucky, because my grandmother was French. She was not like other girls' grandmothers, not just because of the way she spoke, but it was the way she dressed and the way she acted, that made her different. Grandfather had brought her back with him from the war. He was a big man with soft whiskers and a jacket that smelt of pipe smoke. We often called round to see him, my mother and I, and I loved him very much. One day, I was probably about five years old, he wasn't there any more and mother told me he had gone to heaven. I remember feeling very sad that I wouldn't see him again.

After that, Grandma always wore black. She had lots of different dresses, some were made of lace, which were really lovely, but always black. My friends often called in just to look at her. Their grandmas dressed in trousers and bright colours and wore high-heeled shoes. So different from my old-fashioned grandma.

On the mantelpiece in grandmother's sitting room was a box. It was a very beautiful box, but it was locked and nobody was allowed to touch it. It was there one day when we called in, it hadn't been there before. It was quite small and looked a bit out of place alongside the other ornaments on the shelf. It was different from the other beautiful things grandmother had. I often asked her what was in the box, but she always said I would have to wait until I was older.

I was just fourteen, when I found out. I had called in to see her as I often did, on my way home from school. She was sitting in her favourite chair, where she always sat now, but this time she had the box on her lap. She smiled as I came in, and told me to sit down. I knew then I was going to discover the secrets of the box. She opened the lid, took out a leather pouch and carefully emptied the contents on to her lap. There were two folded up letters, a few dried up flowers and other bits and pieces which I didn't recognise.

'This box,' she said, 'is my memory box. When I met your grandfather, I was just a young girl. I lived in a small village in France and he was a soldier fighting for his country.' She went on to tell me how they'd met in the café in the main street and how they liked each other quite a lot. Grandad had to go away the next day, 'to do some more fighting,' she said, but he promised to write when he could.

'These two letters are the only ones which arrived, though he said he had written many,' she smiled. 'But it was the war, so I was lucky to get them. Then the war was over and your grandfather came back to find me. He brought me a rose.' She picked up the dried flower and held it lovingly out to show me. 'And this is a flower from my wedding bouquet, and these are the bootees I knitted for our first born, your mother. Everything in here is a memory.'

She began to put everything back into the pouch, then into the box and closed the lid. 'When I go,' she smiled again, 'I would like to take these with me. I know you love this box, so I would like you to have it to fill with your own memories.'

I was seventeen when Grandmother went to join Grandfather and, as promised, the beautiful box was left to me, empty now. I cherish it. It sits on the shelf in my bedroom, gradually filling up with my own memories, nothing as romantic as my grandmother's, not yet anyway, but perhaps one day I will be able to tell my own granddaughter stories about my memories from the contents of the box.

***

SECRETS

Olivia sat in her usual chair, near enough to the window to see the garden, full of flowers at this time of year. It was a good residential home, well run, the staff were kind as well as being efficient. She was well-looked after, her children had chosen well. Her only complaint was that it was impossible to have a conversation with anyone. Nobody listened to her. Other residents came and sat with her and chatted, and she listened. They told her about their past lives, their children, but she could tell, they really weren't in the least bit interested in anything she had to say.

'How are you, today?' a nurse or one of the many carers, would ask whenever they were passing. She knew there wasn't much point telling them that she was fed up with sitting here and would welcome a bit of conversation, so she always answered, 'Fine, dear, I'm OK,' and then settled back into her chair to watch the flowers grow and listen to the birds sing - and remember.

The only person she could really have a conversation with was her great-grandson, Russ. He had come to see her in the home when he wanted some information for a story he had to write, for homework, about the War. He knew granny had been around then, so he hoped she would have some stories to tell him.

She smiled as she thought back to that first visit. She had thought for many hours about where she should start, and how far she should go, to tell him of her adventures – though at the time they had not felt anything like adventures. There were so many things, so many memories, only good ones; the bad ones were stored away in a box in a part of her brain she never visited, thanks to the psychiatrist she had seen on her return from France.

The first time Russ visited was after school on a Wednesday and when he was seated comfortably in the chair opposite her, his notebook resting on his lap, she started to tell him her story. She told him of how she had been parachuted into France and how she had lived amongst the French people as one of them, and how she had helped the Resistance to hide the pilots who escaped from their planes when they had been shot down, and arranged for them to get back to England. She told him of how she'd hidden in barns amongst the farm animals to escape the German soldiers, and how, eventually, she'd been captured and taken a prisoner herself, and how the British troops had saved her when they finally arrived. She was one of the lucky ones. Many of her friends were killed.

At first, Russ believed every word his great-grandmother told him, but when his teacher and then his parents had gently suggested that it might be that granny was making it all up, he had been very upset. Olivia tried to make him believe it was all true, and he did still talk about it with her, though she felt now, now that he was fifteen, he was just humouring an old lady. But he would find out the truth soon, as would everybody.

Today she'd received her test results from the doctor. It was not good news. Nearing ninety, she supposed she'd had a good innings. She'd lived her life and was quite happy to move on. She hoped her family, at least, would have good memories of her. But now she must tell Sadie, her daughter what the doctors had said. She would leave it up to her to tell anyone else who needed to know. She hoped Russ wouldn't be too upset. He was a good boy. He had all the information about her time in France. Everything was written down in his notebook. Soon he would have the proof that it was all true, not just the ramblings of an old lady. Yesterday her daughter had gone to the bank, to the safety deposit box, to collect the old bag she had made out of a sack all those years ago. The papers which had lain untouched for the past sixty odd years would be proof of the lie she had been living for so long.

Later on they were all coming to visit, as she had asked. Then she would show them everything, the diaries she had kept, the newspaper cuttings she had collected after the war, and the photos. They would get to know the full story. They might not have believed it before, but she hoped the contents of the bag would convince them that everything that Russ had learned from her really was true. She didn't want to wait until after she was gone, she wanted to see their faces, especially when she showed them the photo of her receiving her medal from the King. She hoped they wouldn't be too upset with her. Maybe she should have shown them all the papers and photos sooner, but she hadn't wanted all the fuss it would probably have caused. She put on her glasses and peered at the clock over the door, only a couple more hours and they would be here, she couldn't wait.

***

Barbara Ferris

Roman Remains

It stands high upon the hillside
Forgotten, in decay
Four walls are still left standing
The roof has blown away

The hill behind's eroded
The path in front's a ragged stair
Nobody can reach it now
Few people know it's there

It was built by the Romans
Just by Hadrian's Wall
Did a soldier live there
Big and fit and tall?

Was his family with him
Or was he all alone?
Did he build the house himself
Stone by heavy stone?

There are so many questions
No one seems to know
The birds have taken over
The kestrel and the crows

They build their nests in comfort
Away from human life
They don't care about the Romans
Or the soldier and his wife.

It stands upon the hillside
Forgotten and forlorn
Just four walls and a history
From long before we're born

THE CONDUCTOR

Simon Montgomery was not a happy man. He'd been playing his bassoon with the orchestra for twenty years, man and boy. He'd stood in for the conductor, that silly little Frenchman Jean-Pierre, on many an occasion, when he'd had to make an emergency trip back to Paris, or rush down to London to see someone of great importance. Now, at last, Jean-Pierre was going, goodness knows where, Simon didn't care, and it seemed a foregone conclusion, to him, at any rate, that he would be asked to take over as permanent conductor. But no, the powers that be had given the job to that jumped-up first violinist. That was the last straw for Simon. He wasn't going to stay and be humiliated and laughed at behind his back, no, he was off too.

It wasn't as easy as he had thought it would be to find another orchestra, not one which would appreciate his talents. In fact, after a few weeks and with his bank balance going steadily down, he was getting desperate and would have taken anything offered. But he hadn't reckoned on working with a load of children. The first time he'd stood in the Grammar School assembly hall, in the town he had only vaguely heard of, surrounded by these children, clutching their instrument cases and talking very loudly, he felt he had reached rock bottom. The noise had been horrendous, he wasn't used to that. In fact, he had almost turned round and left. But what other alternative did he have? None, if he wanted to keep the standard of living he had become accustomed to.

At the interview he had been told that the purpose of the job was to form a youth orchestra, one which would be good enough to perform at the Royal Albert Hall at the end of the summer term. They would be competing against orchestras from all over the country. Simon had nine months exactly to prove this could be done.

All the young people had passed an audition, not one organized by him, to qualify for a place in the orchestra, and were considered to be up to standard. All Simon had to do was get them to play the right notes and to keep in time. He had to admit, at the end of the first session, that they weren't bad, and after a month, he was really getting involved and beginning to see that it might just be possible that the noisy crowd of children could become a real orchestra. If nothing else, they were very enthusiastic and worked hard, taking notice of everything they were told. And they always turned up for rehearsals. Simon soon knew them all by name, and their capabilities, and encouraged them to practise and improve their performance. He wasn't slow in telling them how good they all were, and he knew that they would do everything in their power to perform their best for him.

After six months, they gave their first concert, for parents and friends and anyone else who wanted to come. They received a standing ovation and a brilliant write-up in the local paper. The confidence they received from this made them all the more determined to reach their goal. At the end of eight months, he no longer thought of them as children, and he could feel that they respected him. He had managed to convince them that, although it would be wonderful to win, there would be no shame in being runners-up. The main thing was they were going to play their music at the Royal Albert Hall, and they had got there by their own merit.

Now at last the big day had arrived. The coach journey had passed uneventfully, in fact everyone had been very quiet, no doubt all thinking of the task ahead. They were assembled in the waiting area at the Royal Albert Hall. Simon smiled. He hoped they didn't realize how nervous he was. He had listened from the gallery to some of the competition. The standard was high, as he knew it would be, but he was confident his girls and boys were just as good.

The Conductor

Finally, it was their turn. They filed into the Hall, took their places and tuned up their instruments. Simon was even more nervous now, but he smiled down at the young people who had worked so hard to reach this point. He raised his baton, mouthed 'one, two, three' and the magnificent sound of the 1812 Overture filled the Hall. Simon Montgomery was a happy man.

***

THE TRAVELLER

He folds the map and climbs the few feet to a vantage point on the flat rock where he has a good view of the surrounding area. In front of him is the ocean and he can see the bright blues and greens and red of the coral reef just beneath the surface, so many different shades, home to so many different creatures. The water looks calm out there but when it reaches the shore, the waves are wilder as they splash on to the sandy beach. He sees a young family surfing, taking advantage of the waves. There is no one else to be seen. It is the first time he has seen the ocean since leaving the city behind.

He has travelled far, across a whole continent. It has taken him a long time, almost a year, much longer than he had planned. But there was no rush. He has seen places he would never have imagined visiting, sometimes staying for as long as a month. Now he is at his destination, the ocean, as far as he can go, as far as he wanted to go. Every day has been recorded, every place, every event is in his diary. He is on his third notebook. Sometimes, like today, he wonders why he undertook this journey, why could he not have been content to stay in Sydney, going to work, mingling with the hustle and bustle of life. Of course, he knows why. It was his need to get away, away from people, away from everything familiar, to get used to being himself again, just him, now that Louisa, his dear wife, was finally at peace. Well, for whatever reason, he was glad he'd done it.

He had taken the train, hitched rides with truckers, met so many people, interesting people, camped down with the Aborigines, eaten with them round their fires, making himself understood, sometimes just by gestures. Once the men had taken him with them on a hunting trip, but this had been hard to stomach. He understood the need for food, but that was a trip too far.

There had also been many hours, sometimes days, when he had spoken to no one, he relished the solitude. But sometimes it had been hard. He realized early on in his trip how unprepared he was for the wild, red deserts and unrelenting heat of the sun of the Australian outback. He felt the danger there. He knew many people perished in the harsh landscape. But he had taken no unnecessary risks, taken heed of the warnings. On his journey, from the safety of a truck or, occasionally, the train, he saw cattle sheltering under the shade of desert oaks, many miles from any habitations. Who did they belong to, these skinny animals? Perhaps no one, perhaps to an aboriginal family? There were kangaroos and dingoes too, who hid in the dried up bushes to rest and keep cool during the heat of the day. He had been amazed at the number of birds which appeared at the waterholes at dawn and again at dusk, budgerigars, cockatoos, galahs and many more.

He had travelled though the Outback at the end of summer and stayed until the spring. It was only slightly cooler during the winter months, but there were snakes and lizards basking in the sun to enjoy. He noted as many names as he could in his diary. It would all be something to remember when he finally returned home, if he ever did.

Now that he has come to the end of his journey, he will have to decide what to do next. He knows it will be hard to go back to the city and his old life, but what else can he do. He still has money in the bank, but it won't last forever. He looks out across the ocean. The young family have gone and the beach is deserted. He wishes Louisa could have been here with him, she would have loved it, but it was not to be. He still misses her terribly, but the pain has eased. He folds up the map, time to go. He doesn't know what he is going to do yet, but he's ready to face the world again.

***

Barbara Ferris

THE LETTER

I found the letter when I was spring cleaning. My husband's great aunt Emma lived with us for a while, but when she became too much for us to look after, we very reluctantly, but with her consent, found a residential home where she could be looked after by professionals. In the end she had been quite happy to leave us, and soon made friends with the other residents. At 92 years old, she still had most of her faculties and her mind was as alert as ever, in fact we found her a joy to have a conversation with. She loved to tell us about her life, though we never found out why she had never married. On reflection, it was probably because so many young men never returned from the war, and Aunt Emma did seem a bit fussy. She had a good career as a nurse and told us many times that she was quite happy with her life and that a man would have been too much trouble. I don't know if we quite believed her, but that was all we could get out of her.

And now she was gone, we really missed her. We took consolation knowing that she'd had a good life and, as far as we could tell, regretted very little. So now I had to clear out her room. She had taken a lot with her to the home, but there were still a few things to sort out.

I saw the envelope when I opened the drawer of the old bedside cabinet. It was crumpled and yellow with age and addressed to Miss Emma Becket, Aunt Emma. It felt a bit intrusive to read someone else's correspondence, even though she was family, but my curiosity got the better of me. And anyway, I'm sure Emma wouldn't have minded. The envelope contained a neatly folded letter and, what looked like, an old telegram. I carefully removed the letter and smoothed it out. It was written in black ink which had begun to fade, but the handwriting was a beautiful script. I started to read. The letter was dated May 1944.

> My dearest Emma
> Just a few lines to tell you I am still in the land of the living and keeping well. It's been a bit rough lately, our regiment has lost many men, but I am safe for now. I have just received your letter. Even though we've been moving about from place to place, it only took five days to reach me. I was very pleased to get it. I hope you are not working too hard in the hospital. I do admire you. I'm sure all the boys are in love with you, as am I.

There were then a few lines which had been blacked out by the censor. Then it continued.

> We are having very nice weather at present and I hope it continues . . . Soon I hope I will be home and we can start our life together. Fondest love and kisses. Will

This was followed by a line of kisses. I felt the tears in my eyes as I finished reading it. I could imagine Emma receiving the letter and cherishing it, perhaps sleeping with it under her pillow, dreaming of the day when Will would come home. I folded the letter and put it back in the envelope. I would keep it safe. I couldn't bear to read the telegram.

***

Barbara Ferris

THE VAGRANT

I look at the reflection in the shop window. A tall man, a bit stooped now, unshaven and looking as though he could do with a bath. Is that me? The raincoat I'm wearing is a charity shop reject. I found it in a bag outside Oxfam waiting to be taken to the clothes' graveyard. Well, it's warm and doesn't look too bad really, just not up to charity shop standards. It covers the two shirts, two jumpers and the thick corduroy trousers which came from similar sources. Sometimes, when I'm sitting in the warm room of the hostel where they supply hot drinks and a fairly good, if plain, meal I wonder how I ever came to be in this situation.

Not so long ago I had a good job as a warehouse manager which paid well, a pension to look forward to and a nice house, with a bit of a mortgage but quite manageable. I also had a lovely wife and two great children. Now look at me. First of all, the firm I had been with for twenty years folded, and everyone lost their jobs. No golden farewells there, we were lucky to get the wages we were owed. Our pensions disappeared into a black hole and suddenly there were 150 extra people on the unemployment register. It wasn't so bad for the youngsters. They mostly had no ties, no family to keep, no mortgage to pay. And there seemed to be jobs available, lowly paid of course, for anyone under 25 who was willing to do anything. I was 47 with a house and a family, and the few decent jobs available were soon snapped up. The employers had so much choice, and they tended to go for people with degrees rather than experience. Fortunately my wife was working, and we had a little bit of savings, but with all the expense of the house and its upkeep, not to mention the children, money became scarcer and scarcer. Granted I was eligible for social security but that was only about one fifth of what I had been bringing home. It helped a bit, but we were really scraping the barrel.

After a while, I became despondent and gave up all hope of ever working again. I suppose I was depressed, but I wasn't going to admit it and I certainly wasn't going to any doctor. Really, looking back now, my wife was wonderful. She never complained. But I started to argue with her over nothing at all, I shouted at the children so much that they kept well out of my way. Sometimes I didn't see anything of them for days. It got so bad, I was intolerable, I can see that now, and when my wife told me that she couldn't take any more, I stomped out of the house and have never been back. What an idiot I was, still am.

So for the past few months I have been living the life of a vagrant, walking the streets, sleeping wherever there's a space, eating whatever I can or what some kind person gives to me. A lot of the people I see in the shelter spend the little bit of money they get on drink, but I've managed to keep off that, for the moment anyway. And that reflection in the shop window is me. I still find it hard to believe that I have sunk so low, surely there must be a way out. I realize that I have reached rock bottom, there are only two ways to go, try to pull myself together, or give up.

It's three months since I looked in that shop window. I look at the reflection in the mirror. I see a tall man, clean shaven and smartly dressed in neatly pressed clothes. He has a few more lines on his forehead than I remember and is slimmer, but then he could have done with losing a few pounds. I wonder what made me sit on that seat in Oxford City Centre, on that particular day. I wonder what made my wife decide to go shopping that day and walk past the old tramp sitting on that same seat. And I marvel that she turned and looked and recognized the bearded vagrant in the rejected charity shop clothes as the husband who had walked out those months ago. I marvel too that she was not repulsed by my appearance as she sat down beside me and took my hand.

The reflection in the mirror smiles. He looks happy. I still cannot believe that it is me. I have a job now, nothing much but it helps to pay the bills. I have regained my self-esteem. The children are pleased that I am back. And so am I.

THE WILDERNESS

I walk my dog most mornings, time permitting. We do a circular route, up to the common, along the road and then down the lane. Just before the lane merges with the main road, there is an old house, set back from the road, empty now, almost forgotten it seems. I have often wondered who had lived there in the past, in that magnificent house with its arched porchway and the stained glass in the front door, just visible beneath the overgrown ivy. It had been empty for as long as I had lived in the neighbourhood and now had a neglected look, unloved and unwanted.

I shall remember for a long time the day Gus, my extremely naughty dog, slipped his collar and dived into the overgrown tangle of weeds which I'm sure had once been a carefully tended garden. I shouted at him to come back, then waited in vain for him to reappear. I heard his yelp in the distance so, worried that he might be hurt, decided I would have to follow him into the undergrowth.

It was a very large garden, more a field, and I was unsure which way to go. But I had to find the dog, he could be anywhere. So I pushed my way gingerly through the confused mass of vegetation, catching my coat on the brambles on the way, calling his name as I went. Big juicy blackberries hung in abundance from their prickly branches. I felt the crunch of snails beneath my feet and heard the rustle as small creatures, undisturbed for many years, scuttled away to safety. I shouted for him again, but there was no response from my wretched dog – hopefully he was too engrossed in smelling everything rather than lying injured. The trees towered above me, the plants so tall I could see nothing except what was immediately in front. The further in I ventured, the harder it became to make my way through the undergrowth. The ground was covered in shrivelled up crab apples, a few still clinging stubbornly to the dead-looking branches of the tree above. Close by there were dandelions and daisies and other wild flowers pushing their way upwards struggling to find the light.

Still no sign of Gus but I pushed on, repeatedly calling his name. It was a paradise for wildlife, that garden. I stood still and listened, it was like being in the middle of the country rather than in the suburb of a large town. I shut my eyes, I could hear birds gently calling, almost as though they feared to make too much noise in case they were discovered. There were flies now, and butterflies too – was that a red admiral?

There seemed no end to the wilderness. I had no idea where I was or how to get out and there was still no sign of Gus. Perhaps I would be lost forever, they would eventually find me shrivelled up among the decaying fruit. Then I heard a sound, louder than the ones I'd heard earlier, definitely not a mouse. There was a crashing of branches, then there he was, tail wagging and his tongue hanging out. He jumped up and went to put his muddy paws on my now slightly dirty, snagged coat and looked quite offended when told to get down. I fixed his collar firmly back on. 'Well, how do we get out of here,' I asked, expecting him to understand. At the sound of my voice he turned and started to pull me forward.

We reached the road in much quicker time than it had taken me to get completely lost, but not before my dog had sniffed at everything that took his fancy. Back on the pavement at last, I looked down at my muddy shoes, my scratched hands and the vegetation that had attached itself to my coat and seriously wondered if it was really worth having a dog. He must have read my thoughts because he looked up at me with his big brown eyes as if to say 'of course it is'. All I could do was ruffle his ears – then he smiled, yes, I'm sure he did.

THE WORKS' OUTING

Josie walks slowly along the path, the cherry blossom hasn't been out out for many days but already it is beginning to drop, the pink petals drifting gently down forming a carpet beneath her feet. She stops for a moment, listening to the birds hidden in the trees, singing sweetly. There is no other sound, no traffic, no chatter, just perfect.

She feels no guilt at having escaped from the main party, the coach trip that had been planned for weeks to coincide with the Bank Holiday, no guilt at all. They are a noisy lot, all from the office where she works four days a week. Most had made for the nearest pub as soon as the coach had stopped, not unusual for that lot. Josie wasn't looking forward to the journey home, but that was hours away yet. She doubted they had even missed her.

She hadn't really intended to take the trip but the alternative would have been to stay at home with her mother, listening to her moans, running around after her. Mother was quite capable of looking after herself, but if Josie was there she took advantage. Josie knows she's being used but what alternative does she have, after all she is her mother. The outing had been a good excuse to have a bank holiday all to herself for once. She must make the most of it. There are a few hours yet before she has to return to the coach.

She walks further along the path and as she rounds the corner, she sees the house. It looks deserted, the dilapidated door is tightly shut and the windows have been boarded up. As far as she can see, this old house is in a very isolated place, there is no sign of any other buildings, who would have lived here she wondered?

The garden is wild, though the grass has been cut and seems to have been kept under control, who does this? Josie looks around. Maybe someone who had lived here before it had become derelict, someone who has an obsession about keeping the garden as it was when they had lived here themselves. Who knows?

In the middle of the grassy area there are seats, built in on each side of a wooden table. They still look in reasonable condition. Josie sits and makes herself comfortable. An ant scurries along the surface and disappears over the edge of the table, always on the move. Amongst the leaves of the two massive trees at the end of the lawn, if you can call it that, bird boxes, almost invisible, await residents, or have they been and gone? Ivy clambers upwards, its tentacles reaching high up into the branches. The tangled hedge of wild roses fighting its way through the nettles, dock leaves and bindweed, encloses the garden.

Strangely, there is a small patch of garden which has been carefully dug over and seedlings planted. They look like peas, or maybe broad beans, a few lettuces and a few carrots just pushing their way upwards. The whole plot looks well tended.

Josie gets up from her seat and continues her way along the path. She wants to see what is round the next corner, maybe there are other houses, surely this house would have had at least one neighbour. It feels strange, on the one hand it is as though she has gone back in time, yet there are still signs that someone is around, tending the garden, growing the vegetables.

She walks a hundred yards or so and turns down a narrow lane. Suddenly she is back in the present. It seems that the house is not so isolated after all but is situated on the edge of a small village. There is a main road with other houses, shops, even a fish and chip shop, maybe she would go there, she was beginning to feel a bit peckish. And of course, there's a pub. The tables outside are all sprouting brightly coloured umbrellas and all seem to be occupied. She looks again and just too late, realises that the noisy drinkers are the people from the coach that she has been desperately trying to escape from. She must have walked in a full circle.

She turns her back in the hope that she hasn't been seen, but too late, they are calling her name. She sighs, well just one drink then. Then she can escape again, she's sure they won't miss her, anyway she doesn't care if they do.

***

Barbara Johnson

I am a Lancashire lass who, with my husband and two small daughters, left the North West in 1966 but didn't arrive in Northam until Easter 1994, a lot of water having flowed under the bridge during that period. I originally joined a Writing Group in 2004, but saw an advert for Susie's group in September 2011 and wasted no time in joining; a decision I never regretted. (The first Group broke up towards the end of last year, a pity but we remain friends.) I have always liked writing and am amazed at how ideas form, many a time I ask myself 'however did I think about that?' Writing is a wonderful way of keeping the mind active. Also, being in a Group means making new friends. I also love reading, going to the theatre/cinema and music, particularly classical. I am mad about dogs and look forward to welcoming my friend's new dog, Dolly, when Jane brings her home. My two daughters, four grandchildren and two great grandsons live in Hampshire, which means I don't see them as often as I would like. Luckily, I have very good friends and neighbours and, of course, my 'family' at the Writing Group.

BY HOOK OR BY CROOK

Exuding undeserved kindness, the two Medics lean over my inelegant sprawling body. 'Are you alright, dear? What's your name? Can you stand on your own, or would you like a wheelchair?' The questions are fired at me like bullets and echo through my befuddled brain. The answers are barely audible, except for the last one which is screeched beyond decibel range.

'Yes.' 'Irene Mellor.' 'Yes.' 'NOOOOO!'

Embarrassment, humiliation, mortification, call it what you will, but it still sweeps over me, leaving my face feeling so red you could probably fry the proverbial egg on it.

The Medics finish their examination and consult with each other before switching their attention back to me.

'Well, Irene, we'll get you to A&E and have you checked over. That's a nasty bruise coming up on your forehead, might need an X-ray. And that cut on your cheek needs attention, probably a stitch or two. Is there anyone you want to contact?'

'No.' Gosh, that sounded curt. Where are your manners Irene, I chide myself before hastily amending my reply. 'No, no thank you.'

Whilst I realise that I have no choice but to go with them, I hope that with a bit of luck I'll be home before Don gets back from work. He's gone on foot today, that'll add time. Anyway no point bothering him, he'd only panic. Time for explanations later.

Comforted by an arm around each of my shoulders, I let the Medics lead me to the ambulance. By now the 'ghouls' have gathered so I keep my head bowed, and my fingers crossed as I hope and pray that nobody recognises me. Where have all these people come from but, more to the point, where were they when I needed someone?

Eventually, wrapped in the warmth of the obligatory blanket, I allow a few previously unshed tears to trickle down my face, mostly in self-pity, the pain being secondary. Finally, tiredness overcomes me and I drift in and out of a disturbed sleep.

Surprisingly the A&E Department is fairly quiet so I am only in there for just over an hour. Once the X-ray has proved negative and a couple of stitches have been put in my cheek, I am given the all clear and allowed home.

As expected, I arrive back to an empty house. Concerned by my technicolour appearance, the taxi driver insists on holding my arm and accompanying me to the front door. After paying and thanking him, I close the door and flop into the nearest chair with a sigh of relief.

I sit there for a few minutes thinking up an explanation for Don. Finally, in the absence of any evidence to the contrary, I decide to keep it short and simple. Just a straightforward trip on an uneven pavement.

Whilst I'm congratulating myself on the choice of white lie, the doorbell rings. It must be Don - forgotten his key again, a regular occurrence when he doesn't take the car. I struggle to my feet and open the door. No, not Don. Instead two men are standing there.

'Mrs Mellor?' asks the taller and skinnier of the two, waving what looks like an identity card in front of my face, whilst his older companion points a camera at me. Without waiting for a reply, he continues 'Jason White, *Inglefield Herald*. I believe you were involved in an incident at the A2Z Store this afternoon. Care to give us the story?'

I look up at the heavens but divine intervention is taking a day off. I look down at the ground but even this refuses to open up and swallow me.

Desperate for an escape route, I look towards the end of the cul-de-sac but all I can see is Don appearing round the corner. He gives me a wave and quickens his step as he spots the visitors (I can imagine him thinking 'what's she buying this time'). Now there's no alternative but to invite them indoors. After despatching Don into the kitchen to make coffee all round, I take a deep breath, put on my most charming smile for the cameraman and face my inquisitor.

By Hook or By Crook

'Well, it was like this. . .'

Extract from the following week's edition of *The Inglefield Herald:*

> 'It might not have been the 13th, but last Friday was certainly unlucky for one of our local inhabitants when 60 years old Mrs Irene Mellor was involved in a freak accident at the A2Z Store on the Inglefield By-pass.
>
> Unable to find an assistant, diminutive Mrs Mellor was using the handle of her umbrella to reach a box of chocolates on the top of the Confectionery section when her hand slipped as she was distracted by a sudden store announcement. The handle of her umbrella then got caught on the edge of the shelf, dislodging the section and its contents.
>
> Mrs Mellor was taken to hospital but allowed home after treatment to minor cuts and bruises.
>
> A spokesman for the Store admitted that because it was normally a quiet time, there had been an inadequate number of staff on duty and that the damage amounted to about two hundred pounds. However they were dealing with this in-house and wouldn't be taking any further action.
>
> Meanwhile, to avoid any future temptation, Mrs Mellor has promised to exchange her long umbrella for a shorter, collapsible one.
>
> Our photograph shows Mrs Mellor enjoying a box of her favourite chocolates, compliments of this newspaper.'

SHADOWS

We walked on the beach
With long shadows.
Hand in hand, close together
Making footprints that followed.
We didn't need to speak
In this world of our own,
No one else within reach.

We walked over the field
With long shadows.
An old rustic bench beckoned
'Come sit for a while'.
Wrapped in glorious views
We breathed in sweet smelling air
As we stole a quick kiss,
Our love further sealed.

We walked through the wood
With long shadows.
Sun sparkled like dew
through overhead trees,
whilst whispering leaves fell
multi-coloured to the ground.
'Stay, stay' they seemingly cried.
Sadly we smiled: if only we could.

I walk through the town,
Shops are closed, streets are wet.
Dark clouds abound.
But when the rain stops,
A rainbow then follows.
The sun shines again but as I look down
All I can see is just one long shadow.

NOISES OFF

It was more than the noise of the gusty wind that woke me but, still in a sleepy stupor, I couldn't quite determine what it actually was. Had I locked the doors? Were the safety chains on? Windows closed? Yes to all questions. Although there wasn't any reason to worry, I had Tammy with me for the night, and there she was lying on her fleecy bed, out to the world. Anything untoward and she would have been alert and barking furiously; warn off everyone within a mile would my doggy guardian.

I waited - there it was again. Only a little sound, repeated a couple of times. Then silence. I'm not sure what irritated me most, the silence or the noise. Not loud enough for it to have been the wheely bin going on its travels. A mind of its own has the wheely bin, so you never could tell. I put the light on, got out of bed and opened the curtains just a little bit. I allow one of my neighbours to park her car on the hard standing, I could see that but nothing else as recently we had appeared to have become victims of a night time blackout. However, I did admit to offering a silent and belated apology to the Council, when I found the lights had been temporarily out of order, not permanently out of use, and were brightly shining again a few days later. Anyway, opening the curtains a little more, and pushing aside the nets I managed to squint down into the corner where I could just make out a shape. At least the bin was still in its rightful place.

It made me think back to a similar windy night three or four years ago when it had decided to go walkabout. The noise then was a full-scale clatter, as the lid was joining in the chorus by flapping up and down. I could hear it slowly making its way down the hard standing. Then it drunkenly fell over onto the edge of the pavement before spewing up its indigestible cardboard contents, for the wind to scatter in all directions through the darkness. It was at a time when all cardboard was put in the bin, not like the present day when cardboard is collected separately in brown bags, so anyone passing on that early morning would have been left in no doubt as to what I have for my breakfast, possibly lunch/tea as well in some cases but also, shock! horror!, what my bra size is. By the time I was on the scene, I was only able to rescue a small part of my recycling. As the relevant end of the street meets the main road to Appledore, I can only assume that is the direction the majority headed towards. Lucky Appledore! Anyway reminiscing didn't solve anything and I was very tired.

Tammy had finally wakened, lifted her head and looked at me, obviously expecting to join in the fun. Instead I gave her a cuddle and told her to go back to sleep, which, by then, is all I wanted to do as well.

Morning came, and with it Jane to collect Tammy, leaving me to study the hard standing. With my neighbour having already driven off, there just remained the debris. The standing is quite wide, on a slight slope and at an angle. Apart from being regularly used as a bin by all and sundry passing by, rubbish is also blown onto it then trapped under any parked car as well as behind and between all the flower pots.

I cleared up - none of it was mine - a piece of newspaper (don't read that), empty packet of cigs (don't smoke), a choccy wrapper (don't like that), empty envelope (hey ho, someone's lost a shopping list), half a chewed-up ball (Tammy doesn't play with balls) and a Red Bull can (ugh, certainly don't drink that), although I had more than just a suspicion that had been the cause of the noise.

As I always say, you never know what you might find, particularly after a very windy night.

***

Barbara Johnson

THE SIXTH SENSE

From turned on tap to waiting glass,
Taste it
Water
Thirst refreshing and life saving.

Over waterfalls, down to valleys,
Hear it
Water
Trickling, gushing.

Overhead skies start to darken,
See it
Water
From bruised clouds raining.

Across the ocean to horizon,
Smell it
Water
Ozone salty, ebbing, flowing.

Come end of day and tired body,
Touch it
Water
Relaxing, cleansing.

In all its guises which surround us,
Fear it
Water
Devastation and life taking.

A BIT OF A SONG AND DANCE

'A 'you're adorable, 'B' you're so beautiful. . .' sang Harold Potts in his tuneless baritone voice, at the same time dancing around the room in an exaggerated fashion. He'd been watching one of his favourite videos and had to admit that Morecambe & Wise looked more the part than he did as they'd twirled around the stage with the real Angela Rippon, and not an overstuffed gold-coloured satin cushion.

Morecambe & Wise. His eyes misted over. How he loved and admired them. He had all of their work together with most of the other old acts and popular series of the 60s, 70s and 80s. Not for him the blood and gore of modern drama, or the foul language of a lot of these so-called stand up comedians. No, give him the oldies any time.

Nothing like hearing, 'You stupid boy, Pike!' or '4 candles?' to cheer him up on a bad day. His worries would soon fade away. Actually, a glance at the clock made him realise that he needed cheering up right now. It was his birthday and the family visit was imminent. 'Be with you about 2,' his daughter had announced when she had phoned him that morning. 'We'll bring the food as usual.' Always the same words, always the same food. Tuna, egg and sometimes a third choice of sandwich, the plainest cake possible, no cream or gooey confection for Harold, and a bottle of non-alcoholic wine. Luckily they only visited Christmas Day, Good Friday, Harold's birthday and at such times when they were hard-up; although these visits came under the heading of, 'Just in the area, thought we'd pop in.' Despite a 200 mile space between them.

Harold made a face and dashed up to his bedroom. Better put on something more appropriate, he thought, dragging a pair of traditional trousers and a severe looking check shirt from their hangers. Pity the family never appreciated the more outlandish outfits. His choice of clothing topped their list of 'Father's Strange Behaviour', a list which was frequently added to as proof, in case it ever came necessary to have him certified. Something they were always threatening to do. It never occurred to them that in Harold's world, he was the only sane one amongst them.

When the doorbell finally rang, he was waiting ramrod straight on his old settee in the gloomy sitting room. The same old sepia photos of five generations ago, great granddad, great aunty Maggie or somebody, all lining the walls in their heavy, ugly gilt frames. An equally old fashioned 14 inch black and white telly and ancient wireless were pushed into the corner, Everything in the room had been handed down over the years. Family, that was what it was all about, so called heirlooms. What a load of pretentious rot.

The family let themselves in. First Margaret, his daughter, with Clive, her husband, trailing behind with a couple of plastic bags, then Robert, his son with his second wife, Melissa, leading to lots of air kissing and tightly grasped hand shaking. Harold winced. None of it meant anything; he wished they'd leave out the amateur dramatics and just say 'hello'. Four of his grandchildren trailed behind, managing to smile whilst trying hard not to look too bored and wishing they were anywhere else but here. Harold winced again. Finally his four great grandchildren consisting of three teenagers and a baby. The older ones, staring down at the floor, muttered something which Harold didn't understand. He just hoped it wasn't too rude. Then they practically became non-existent, as they morphed into some form of voiceless alien life, dependent on something called iPhones and 'tablets' as they spent the rest of the afternoon twittering, tweeting and texting each other. 'What's happened to conversation?' thought Harold. He worried about today's youth. Meanwhile, disturbed by all the movement, the baby opened her eyes, looked him up and down in the way that only babies do, blew a raspberry and went back to sleep. Harold winced even more visibly, feeling somewhat under-whelmed by the occasion.

Margaret suddenly remembered why they'd called. 'Happy Birthday, father!' Not dad, pa or even daddy, his daughter was always correct, a pseudo-snob. They'd all forgotten their northern roots, after his daughter had followed her brother and moved to the south-east.

'See you've still got the old TV,' his son commented approvingly. 'If it ain't broke, don't fix it, eh? Can't keep spending our inheritance. Nudge, nudge and all that.' He always considered this his little joke and trotted it out on every occasion. His loud laugh echoed round the room as he jutted Harold in the ribs with his elbow. Harold outwardly smiled, but inwardly seethed.

'Mind you this rug is new, bit wasteful if you ask me,' sniffed Margaret as she spread the food on the table. Where's the old one? Hope you haven't thrown it out, part of our heritage, the real thing, great-great-grandfather brought it back from Persia.'

Harold swore under his breath, in his haste he'd forgotten to swap them, bad mistake on his part. Although when Harold thought about the worn, threadbare rug, or rag as he preferred to call it, and the number of times his life had been at risk from tripping over it, the best place for it was really the tip.

'I must admit, father, that the place is looking very spic and span.' This was praise indeed from the ever critical Margaret. Harold nodded, but didn't bother to enlighten her, just quietly thanked Him up above for introducing the obliging Mrs Etherington into his life. Mrs E came five days a week, although only two were officially related to household activities.

And so they carried on eating, in silence. A piece of dry sandwich stuck in Harold's throat. He longed for a pint. Still, not to worry they'd soon be gone. They never stayed more than two hours. The thought cheered him up immensely.

True to form, on the dot of four, they upped sticks, packed the remaining food and, with more air kissing and hand shaking, made to leave. Harold waited patiently.

Last in the queue to leave, his daughter handed him a small parcel. 'Bet you thought we'd forgotten!' It was Margaret's annual ritual; even she had her little joke.

Harold smiled through gritted teeth, 'Thank you all very much. And thank you for coming. Nice to have seen you again. Look forward to next time. Goodbye.' As usual, his well practised speech fell on deaf ears as they were already slamming the doors of their respective posh cars.

Harold gave a big sigh of relief and went back indoors. Now his birthday could really begin. He ran upstairs two at a time and unlocked the bedroom door. This was where he really lived. The four bedrooms had been knocked into one huge apartment which was always kept locked. So far his family were unaware of the alterations - they showed no interest or curiosity in how he lived. Their only concern was the value of 'their inheritance' which, to them, apart from the house, consisted solely of their so-called precious heirlooms.

Little did they realise that this was where the money was. Not hidden, but on show in his converted apartment. The bedroom was luxurious, the canopied double bed covered by a vivid multi-coloured heavy cotton bedspread and matching pillow shams took centre stage. A crystal chandelier hung above. The bedroom furniture was expensive, made-to-order oak. Expensive china ornaments were dotted all around whilst original modern art dominated the wall space.

After a quick shower in the marbled en-suite, mainly to get rid of the lingering smells of the overdone perfume and aftershave, Harold padded over to the wardrobe. The clothes he brought out were in complete contrast to what he had been wearing. The traditional, now back on hangers, was replaced by the modern – an outfit that many a younger man would envy. He finally pulled his shirt collar over the neck edge of the quilted body warmer and checked his image in the long free-standing mirror. He might be in his mid-seventies but he had no intention of either dressing or behaving like it.

He walked out of the bedroom, through the ultra-modern kitchen, into a lounge exuding wealth, the majority of which came from the contents of the bookshelf which ran along a whole wall. He ran his hand along them. His books, first editions, all bearing his own signature, not that of his alter ego.

'Edward Whittaker' had served him well over the years whilst Harold Potts, author and acclaimed Childrens' writer remained incognito and out of the public eye. By now even the media had given up trying to locate him. He had always been keen on scribbling the odd piece and after selling a collection of articles to the local newspaper in his earlier years, had turned to serious writing when his children left home and more so since his wife had asked for a divorce and gone off with a toy-boy.

His family would never know about his secret life. When he left this mortal coil, he had arranged with his solicitor and closest friends that the apartment would revert to four bedrooms with all the original furniture, currently in storage, replaced. His books would be given to the Childrens' Hospital, for keeping or selling, and all other contents would be disposed of as agreed by friends. The house by right, together with the so-called heirlooms, which had been valued and deemed worthless before going into store, would go to his family. That is what they were waiting for, that is what they would get. Anyway better things to do. A party to attend.

After carefully locking up, he strode along the street to his local. His friends were obviously already there, he could hear them talking and laughing. He entered to a great cheer. 'This is more like it,' he thought, happily responding to all the hugs and kisses. 'A proper greeting.' His friends were long standing and very loyal. They had kept his secret well. They were proud of him 'you've just got a well paid job' they'd told him unenvyingly. He never showed off, money he spent on himself and his home was spent privately. And when they were all out together, they were all equal and he only allowed himself to take and spend the same. Except for special occasions like this. 'Drinks all round,' he shouted before pulling the very delectable Angela Etherington to her feet and on to the small dance floor.

Holding her close, he twirled her round and round, whilst his favourite song resounded throughout the room. 'A' you're adorable, 'B' you're so beautiful'.

Barbara Johnson

SPLISH SPLASH

The rain that falls is hardly a splatter,
but to young Tommy Robbins
this just doesn't matter.
As face all aglow
and clothes in a muddle,
he floats his two sticks
on what now is a puddle.

The rain that falls is simply a shower,
quenching the thirst
of each tree, plant and flower.
Still schoolboy Tom Robbins,
of the outdoors so fond,
sails his toy yacht
on what now is a pond.

The rain that falls is a torrential downpour,
dark and menacing,
threatening more.
Through this Thomas Robbins,
taking a break,
climbs into his dinghy
on what now is a lake.

Splish Splash

The rain that falls is a raging storm
and on the horizon
thunderclouds form.
Whilst Able Seaman T. Robbins,
footloose and free,
boards his first ship
on what now is a sea.

The rain that falls is turning to snow,
though nothing can spoil
celebrations below.
Where Captain Robbins RN,
so full of emotion,
salutes his brave crew
on what now is an ocean.

No rain falls, just tears of sorrow.
For the late Admiral Robbins
there is no tomorrow.
As loving hands,
to muted strains of the band,
gently lay him to rest
on what now is dry land.

***

Barbara Johnson

THE DEEP SECRET

Pushing my chair away from the table, I look towards my wife. 'Won't be long, love. Just off to tidy up Mrs Bradley's garden. She'll be back from her sister's on Sunday.'

As Janey starts to clear the breakfast things away, I hover momentarily at the back door and, as usual, admire the effortless way she moves - her trim, aproned figure reflected in the spotlessly clean kitchen. You wouldn't think she is nearly seventy; looks after herself well does my Janey.

Opening the door, I step out into the garden. Immediately I am overpowered by the fragrance from the abundance of roses and other sweet smelling summer flowers. Here 'tempus' does not normally 'fugit' and there is usually time to stand and stare but, today, there is something more imminent and even more important than Mrs Bradley to think about - the Annual Flower Show.

I stop to carefully inspect the heavily scented dark red petals of the glorious Deep Secret, especially groomed to win the Best Rose in Show. Although over the years I have won various awards, this will be my last chance to win the coveted Cup and I am determined to beat my old rivals. Next year we will be living in a town far away from here but, even with the bonus of having our married daughter and grandchildren closer at hand, I shudder at the thought of leaving behind what has been home for most of our married life. I will miss the people, the village itself and surrounding countryside beyond words. But neither of us are getting any younger and it was a bitter blow when I had to stop driving due to deteriorating eyesight, even more so with the closure of so many local shops and the ever decreasing bus service. At least Janey will be happy - she's never complained about being out in the sticks but my wife is a real townie at heart.

Reluctantly putting aside thoughts of the Show, I go through the broken gate. Should have repaired it long ago but, like everything else not related to the garden, it's way down the list. As I turn to go into the lane leading to Hudson's Farm, I sense something is wrong. The sheep are making an unholy din almost drowning out the sound of barking.

Suddenly, a moving carpet of curly fleece appears round the corner as the sheep push and shove their way towards me. I know that Frank Hudson's older and more experienced collie has been out of action with an injured foot and it is obvious that her younger replacement is totally out of her depth in dealing with the unruly mob. They jostle against me, spilling through the gate and into the garden. The precious rose bushes are shaken and bent in the onslaught, the ground becomes covered in mashed up multi-coloured petals.

By now Janey, already aware of the disturbance, dashes outside, ineffectively waving her apron and making shooing noises.

'I've rung the farm, someone's on the way,' she manages to gasp between tears.

Once on the scene, a very red-faced and apologetic Frank soon has the situation under control, eventually leaving me and Janey to survey the damage in silence. My dreams are shattered.

Arms round each other we go back indoors, tears still pouring down Janey's face although, in the end, she is the first to recover.

'Oh, Ted love, the poor roses. All that work you've put in. What about the Show, what will you do now?'

I cannot bear the disappointment - the thought of winning the Show has become unimportant compared with not being able to enter it at all.

Then out of the blue an idea starts to form. Mrs Bradley has a Deep Secret. Could I? Dare I? Nobody would know but me.

Well, and Janey of course. I'll have to think up a way of getting round her.

'Won't be long', I tell my wife for the second time that morning, 'Must get off to Mrs Bradley's. No good standing around here moping. I'll clear up later.'

By the time I reach Mrs Bradley's, I have convinced myself that somehow the rose belongs to me anyway. Although she had bought it, didn't I choose and plant it. And haven't I fed, pruned, watered and cared for it since. Therefore I have no conscience and feel quite justified in carrying out my plan. I examine each bloom in turn until I find the right one. It's not as perfect as my own was but it is still worthy of a prize and I reach for my secateurs. Finally, with the rose safely tucked away, I return home to face Janey.

The following morning, I wake early. A blue sky and bright sunshine herald the day of the Show. I'd tossed and turned most of the night, after having eventually found the nerve to confess and face up to the full force of my wife's wrath. She wasn't best pleased - ranting and raving for the best part of an hour before reluctantly promising to keep quiet.

At mid-day we make our way to the Village Hall. Crowds are already gathering and I try to hide my nervousness as I greet friends and fellow exhibitors. I manage to hold myself together but, as I start to arrange my display, guilt overcomes me. I feel as though Mrs Bradley is watching, her eyes boring into me accusingly. Then I get an even bigger shock as I look up and realise that she actually is, and waving frantically across the table.

'Good luck, Ted. Got back late last night. Couldn't miss the Show. Had to come and cheer you on.'

Can I really go through with this? But, by now, we have reached the point of no return. The judges are assembled and begin their walk round the room, inspecting all the entries before drawing up a short list. The routine begins again - slowly and critically they stop in front of each rose before finally making up their minds.

My heart beats even faster as we wait for the ultimate decision. At last the senior judge steps forward. Third, second -

where will the longed for first prize go. I feel Janey's hand tighten round mine. We hold our breath as the judge picks up the card and leans forward to place it in front of my Deep Secret.

At the same time, instead of the anticipated applause, there is a horrified gasp as, without warning, every precious petal of my stolen rose falls as one, covering the white cloth in a velvety dark red perfume.

***

THE JUDAS STEP

I lower myself onto the step which gives back its stored warmth from the sickly winter sun and I ponder, not for the first time, the paradox of its purpose; it is both the way in and the way out.

Looking around as I stroke the smooth grey stone, I see my familiar friends - to the left and right of me - there they are, identical steps belonging to what was a row of identical houses. Houses which many years ago were full of life and promise but today are just sightless, headless and soulless skeletons - their windows smashed, roofs missing and insides stripped bare.

For over a century they had been filled with generations of the same families who had grown up and probably died there and I belonged to one of them. I had played in this street come rain or shine and, regardless of all the dire warnings from ma, I would insist on jumping in every puddle until I was soaked to the skin or stretching myself out on the step until my face and arms were burning with pain.

Apart from the company of my own siblings - three brothers and two sisters - all older than me, I was part of the gang. All the kids in the street played together. O.K. there was the occasional falling out, like over who would be the 'goodie' or the 'baddie', or whose turn it was to be 'top dog'. But most scuffles or arguments would be sorted out within minutes rather than hours. Often my sisters would bully me into playing with them. This was when the step came into its own. Depending on the current pastime, it would be converted into a school, a stage, a tea party, or a hospital. As a result I was included with a motley crew of dolls and, in turn, became a pupil, singer, visitor or nurse. My patience knew no bounds even though I would sooner have been playing hide and seek, football or any other boyish game.

Sometimes, particularly on a fine summer's evening, even ma and the neighbours would come out and take turns holding a rope, whilst girls, boys and even adults would skip to their heart's content. The memory of caring and camaraderie remains with me to this day.

Inevitably, things changed. The gang grew up. Whilst some went on to higher education, the others - like me - couldn't wait to get a job and start earning.

So started the next part of my life.

I worked really hard as I enjoyed my job with the local Council. By the time I was twenty-two and planning my wedding, I had been promoted twice in quick succession and was beginning to be noticed by senior management.

I had married on a sunny June day and, nostalgically, insisted on standing on the step for photographs. Neighbours had cheered me on my way, not just to the Church but to the new life I would be starting a few miles away.

I still made regular visits back to my old street, taking with me one, then two and finally three daughters. They quickly learned to mix with all the other children who, like them, made regular visits to their grandparents, and played on the step.

Then had come the announcement, a bitter blow. The street and surrounding area was designated as part of a redevelopment plan. No amount of petitioning or protest marching could change the planners' minds. The decision had been made and the street would be razed to the ground to make way for a new supermarket and connecting road.

Everyone was to be re-homed, but not necessarily in the same part of the town. Because of ill-health, ma and pa were moved to a small bungalow on the edge of the countryside. Although they were disappointed not to be nearer their long standing friends, they soon settled but, hopefully, will never find out the price I had to pay for their segregation.

Just three months later, but too late to make any difference, plans for the supermarket hit a major problem and were finally quashed.

For the past twelve years, on that date, I have made a visit to the street to sit on the step, but now no more. Finally, a new housing development is to take place. It is time to say farewell.

I get to my feet, but before walking away there is something I must confess. Facing the houses, they stare back at me with their empty eyes. In that moment I realise that they have always known the truth. So really there is no need to say anything although the guilt will remain with me forever. That is my punishment. For whilst I hadn't personally signed their death warrant all those years ago, I had been responsible for casting the deciding vote which had sealed their fate.

I try to say goodbye, but in doing so, the atmosphere changes, the eyes that now stare back at me are oozing with hatred. The sky darkens even more so and the once gentle snowflakes turn into a full-scale snowstorm. Malicious laughter follows me as I stumble onto the soft ground, dropping my car keys in the process. I fumble around in vain. It's like a cruel game is being played as I see the keys and then they disappear from my reach. Over and over again. All the while I am rapidly becoming covered in white. I can no longer move, I can no longer shout. Voices take over, taunting me, whilst the laughter has now turned to a crazed sound, going round and round in my head. My eyes fill with frozen tears. I can't feel any more.

But I hear them clearly now... 'G o o d b y e   J u d a s...'

THE SILENCE

My heart starts to pound,
the signs are returning,
My head starts to throb,
I can feel my skin burning.

Panic runs through my body.
'Go away, go away.
Please don't come near me',
is all I can say.

I know what to do
but can I manage to do it
before this thing takes over
and I fall into the pit.

I pull on my coat,
put on my shoes.
I slam the door shut.
There's no time to lose.

I run down the street,
then through the park.
I must get there quick
before surrounded by dark.

Just cross the road,
and I've finally made it.
All I want is here, if I stand
and don't sit.

Barbara Johnson

I lean over the railings
and breathe in the air.
Crowds of people walk by me
but what do I care.

I neither see them nor hear them
as I stare into space.
Light returns to heal me,
I feel the sun on my face.

I don't need tablets, medicine,
Acupuncture or yoga.
My medication is free,
it needs no prescription.

I just look at the sea
and feel its compassion.
For what I have found
there is no description.

YESTERDAY TOMORROW

The woman stirs, stretches her body, opens her eyes, and smiles, immediately directing her glance across the bedroom at the picture.

When she had seen it, propped up near the doorway of the local Gallery, she hadn't hesitated, unable to take her eyes away from it. It was meant to be hers. A print, she couldn't have afforded the original. A nothing picture. Simplicity in itself. An unopened white cowslip, with three pale pink and white leaves, surrounded by an ethereal pale grey cloud, with a pale blue sky filling in the remaining space. The lady in the Gallery had framed, delivered and even hung it, not knowing then what effect it would have on the new owner's life.

Day after day, week after week the woman sits in the facing bedroom chair and stares. The picture whispers and cajoles, inviting stories of her life. She tells it tales of her past, sharing both sad and happy memories and, sometimes, secrets that even her family and closest friends are unaware of. She is completely obsessed. It has taken over her life.

Her thoughts get drawn in deeper and deeper. It is such a fragile piece of art but it has a strength that frightens her, and at times it is impossible to summon up enough strength to walk away. Even so, she enjoys being trapped in this cosy world of the past where she doesn't have to worry what the future will bring.

However, within this time, she has almost forgotten her other picture, painted by her husband and once loved as much as her latest acquisition.

She doesn't look at it very often, but she looks now - a large painting of a jug of vibrant pink roses, standing in the centre of a highly polished table. It, too, once spoke to her but in a stronger tone enriched with optimism. Today it looks at her sadly and questionably murmurs softly 'Why do you live for yesterday? Live your life and enjoy tomorrow.' She looks at it as though she has never seen it before. However, it is true, the picture could become a threat so she makes her decision. The following day, she takes the picture down and throws it to the back of the garden shed.

As time goes by, old and frail, friendless and lonely, the woman still wakes every morning and looks at her inanimate but only companion. Whilst, still confined in their prison, the exiled roses have wilted, the faded petals of their once fragrant flowers now strewn across the rotting wooden table.

***

FLIGHT
(a short story based on fact)

The sudden silence, the larger birds cluster together to take shelter under bushes and hedges. The smaller ones pace themselves ready to fly upwards out of danger. Everything comes to a halt. The garden closes down.

Then out of the clear blue sky, with outstretched wings supporting his short plump body, the sparrowhawk appears. With a movement that is swift, straight and stunning, he swoops towards his chosen prey, not one of the birds trying unsuccessfully to hide but the young robin, distracted by the food on the bird table and so totally unaware of any looming disaster. Until too late, it is caught in the shadow of its predator. It trembles in fear and awaits certain death. However, help is at hand from a totally unexpected source.

With ear-splitting squawking and ruffling of feathers, the five hens rush to the aid of the unfortunate victim and courageously jump and flutter round the villain of the piece as they try to distract him. He is just out of reach of all the pecking but their joint efforts pay off and, obviously not hungry enough to bother any further with the battle, he succumbs to defeat. He flies off, but with a look in his eyes that threatens he'll be back. After all, as nature decrees, all birds need to eat.

THE HOUSE

The house stands lonely and neglected on the precarious cliff edge, an eerie silhouette against the evening's glow. It knows little else nowadays.

Gone are the days of glory and constant companionship when, full of life, its vibrancy attracted visitors all year round. It saw continuous days of summer sunshine when laughter filled the air and families would leave its confines and spend their time on the golden beached surroundings. When children hunted for crabs in sparkling pools and bravely ventured to paddle on the edge of the ocean's chilly water, sometimes jumping haphazardly over the incoming waves. At night, bathed in moonlight, it would lie in wait for the wild relentless sea when white horses would rush in, only to be battered against the huge rocks, leaving outstretched tentacles to curl between pebbles as they struggled to reach the remaining grains of sand.

Now only questions abound. What will happen now as bricks and mortar wait in silence to learn their fate? Will the house be saved by humanity, its skeleton nursed back to health and slowly returned to its former splendour for a new generation to visit and admire? Will its eyes be stripped of the heavy wooden bandages which blind it from the outside world so letting the sun once again shine through to spread brightness and warmth within the bare, cold and damp cobwebbed rooms?

As for the garden, overrun by weeds and brambles, now providing a natural habitat for wildlife, will this one day be transformed and re-created into the once well-cut lawn with surrounding borders of sweet smelling colour?

Or, sadly, will it signify the end of something wonderful and the house be left unloved and untended until, in despair, it becomes ready to surrender, slowly crumbling away until one final storm sends it over the edge into a patiently waiting watery grave, lost forever to future generations who will never witness its eerie silhouette, but fondly remembered by the living as 'the haunted house'.

***

Diana Warmington

For most of my working life I was a Shorthand Typist, but in my leisure time I was often elected Secretary of many sport and art-related organisations, writing the Minutes and Newsletters for the membership. They were then the main purpose of my writing. But I have many interests, including archaeology, music, choral singing and local history, plus a love of the countryside and North Devon where I live, and all of these are stored in my subconscious. Joining a Creative Writing group has encouraged me to use these experiences as well as my imagination. The regular meetings with the group also stimulate ideas to inspire my work. I have used memories from my life to assemble a poem, a scene or short story, and have found it a most enjoyable and relaxing experience.

A LIFE

A boy is born
At break of dawn
A bonny lad
For Mum and Dad
They name him Joe
And watch him grow
He starts to walk
And then to talk
Off to school
That is the rule
Learns to read
And picks up speed
Learns to write
To his delight
Sport is best
No time for rest
Growing fast
Childhood past
Off to College
To gain more knowledge
Joe leaves his home
Begins to roam
To see the world
The lands unfurled
Comes home at last
And finds a lass
Down on one knee
Will you marry me?
Wedding bells ring
What will they bring?
A happy home
With babes to come

Diana Warmington

Successful career
Finances all clear
With love and friends
Their joy depends
The children grow
And start to show
That leaving the nest
Will be for the best
Joe and his wife
Begin their new life
With only each other
To manage together
New hobbies to find
Instead of the grind
Of endless tedium
With no happy medium
Retirement at last
They look at the past
And smile they might
They did things right
Joe lost his wife
The love of his life
He followed soon after
Was no good without her
Their children stood round
The graves in the ground
Gave thanks and were glad
They had that Mum and Dad.

***

BEACHCOMBING

'Now, look here, Nellie, are you sure it came in here? I can't see anything,' Doris's boots crunched over the stones, her eyes fixed downwards.

'Of course I am, Doris. Old Sam up on the hill saw it for himself, out walking his dog late last night. He said it definitely came into this cove, so here they must be.'

'Well, all right, but it's like looking for a needle in a haystack for such small things in these stones,' wailed her friend.

'Ah yes, but it'll be worth it when we do find them,' reassured Nellie. 'Look here. We'll do it this way. We'll walk up a couple of yards till we come to the rock or the edge of the water, up one way, and down the next. Then move on a couple of yards beside that, up and down each stretch till we find something. Do you see what I mean?'

'All right, just as you say, but it had better be worth it, my back's giving me gip already,' Doris sighed, straightening up to relieve the pain. 'And the tide's coming in, so we'd better watch out for that. I'm no swimmer and running up that cliff path won't do me any good.'

As agreed, together they marched slowly up and down the stony beach, eyes cast down, searching, all the time hoping to see something glinting, something different from the rounded pebbles that endlessly covered this hidden cove.

After ten minutes' silent walking, staring at the ground, Doris was getting tired of it.

'Can we have a rest, Nell, my neck's hurting now, as well as my back, I can't do much more, old thing.' She leant against the rock, and slowly slid down until she was sitting on the stones. She wondered if she would be able to get up again.

'Well, you have your rest, old thing, but I shall carry on.' Nellie strode on, up and down the beach, her basket held ready for the pickings she was hoping to find. Time passed. Doris dozed. Nellie walked, until she had covered almost half the beach. After a while, and with an empty basket, she joined Doris at the rock face, leaning back to rest.

'I don't know what to think,' she mused. 'Sam said he saw the ship coming near and sitting offshore. It was dark and the sea was very rough. A dinghy was lowered and two fellows rowed towards the beach. They dragged their boat onto the shingle and unloaded some open-top boxes which they carried towards the cliff path. They returned for another. Sam saw it clearly, and said there was something shining in the boxes. Now the path is at this end, and if they did drop anything, it would be right here, or across from the edge of the water. Come on, Doris, let's give it another go. If we find any, we'll be in clover! If we don't do it today, Sam will have told everyone and they'll all be down here!'

Doris struggled to her feet, with a helping hand from Nellie. 'Good thing I'm your friend, Nell, I wouldn't do this for everyone.' She reluctantly joined Nellie, and they continued the search, up and down, up and down. It was quiet except for the crunch of their boots on the stones, and the sucking sound of the waves creeping forward and back, getting surreptitiously nearer to the beach-combers.

'Look! There!' cried Doris. 'What's that? I think I've found one!' She pointed to something shining between the stones. Something small and round shone in the light. Nellie turned and stared down. Pointing her finger at the spot in order to follow Doris's sign, she knelt down, her bulky clothes hampering her, her basket falling onto the stones beside her.

'By golly, you're right! It's a silver doubloon, it really is! Oh, and here's another! Doris, this is a trail, they must have lost a few when they got to the cliff path. Bonanza! Hooray!' Nellie got up, with difficulty, and held up her hands to heaven. 'Come on, Doris, it's harvest time!'

Now they had got their eye in, they began to find more silver coins; some they lost, dropping through the stones as they gingerly picked them up, the sand beneath sometimes claiming the booty the two women were desperate to retrieve. The basket was lined with felt, and the coins chinked sweetly together as Nellie foraged for more. She gazed down at them occasionally, and stopped to examine them. She saw the design of the cross, and strange letters embossed in the spaces. Some had been cut and trimmed, and she wondered why people would do such a thing to real money.

'Just look at these, Doris, aren't they fine! The sea has kept them bright, they really look like treasure. Aren't we the lucky ones! Those sailors were a bit careless with their load, dropping this lot. How many have we got?'

Doris examined the loot, admiring the patterns and figures. She counted, cradling them in her hands as she did so. 'Aren't they lovely, Nellie, not bad for a few hours' work, was it? Twenty two in all.'

'How much do you think they're worth? Are we going to be rich, then?'

'Can't say yet, love,' Nellie was cautious. 'We'll keep them a while, in case this comes up on the news. If it was something outside the law, like a shipwreck being ransacked – and it looks like it, those fellows coming in at night, and all that. Let's call it a day, and get them home.'

Doris was pleased to hear that said, and together they made for the cliff path, winding upward to the pasture, all the while looking at their feet to see if any more coins had been spilled on the way. They found just one in the grass near the top, obviously overlooked by the men as they climbed.

'Twenty three now, Nellie, even better. Cover them up with your gloves, or something, we don't want people seeing them when we pass by those houses.'

They strolled nonchalantly past the dwellings, trying to look inconspicuous. They didn't see anyone, but someone had seen them.

Their home, which they shared, was set back from the road. Just a chalet with a veranda at the front. It had a sitting room, a kitchen, a bathroom and two bedrooms. They tended a small garden front and back, with a few windswept shrubs, a vegetable patch, an outside shed and a greenhouse. Their lives were simple, frugal, and informal. They shared everything, including any money they had, which wasn't much, just pensions. Neither had any children, or relatives they cared about.

Nellie cooked and cleaned, did the shopping and the garden. Doris read a lot, dusted occasionally and sometimes polished the furniture when there was nothing else to do. She arranged flowers rather nicely, too.

That day, returning to their home, Nellie took off her boots, hung up her spotted anorak, and went into her bedroom. Crossing to the window sill, she took down the wooden tea caddy she had inherited from her Mother, took out its key, and tipped the coins into the wells. She replaced the inside lids, closed down the top and locked it. 'There,' she nodded to herself. 'That will do for now.'

Doris came in and asked if there was a cup of tea going. Nellie sighed, and went to put the kettle on. Doris had taken off her boots and red coat, and was relaxing in her favourite chair in the sitting room and waited while Nellie brought in the tea tray, and some walnut cake. They relaxed together, and chatted excitedly about their find, hoping old Sam hadn't told anyone else. He was an old friend, and probably thought these two old dears wouldn't even think of going down that cliff path to find something he wasn't even sure about. They laughed about that, congratulating each other on their daring adventure.

'Can I just have one of those coins to look at, Nellie?' asked Doris. 'I really would like to see them properly in the light.' 'Well, all right, Doris,' agreed Nellie. 'But it must go back in the caddy afterwards, we can't be too careful.' Doris nodded, and waited while Nell fetched a coin for her to hold.

'I wonder if I looked these up in one of our Encyclopaedias, I would learn something about them?' Doris rose and looked in the bookcase.

'All right, but be quick,' Nell was getting nervous. Doris found her copy, and leafing through, found some photographs of Spanish doubloons. 'Yes, we've definitely got the real thing, Nellie. Just like the picture.' They sat side by side, comparing the coin with the photograph, and laughed and laughed.

A knock on the door made them look up. Startled, Nellie rose, stuffing the coin into her trouser pocket, and closing Doris's book. She opened the door and found a Police Constable standing there.

'Can I help you, officer?' asked Nellie, sweetly. 'I think you can, madam. I understand you've been on the beach today. Were you looking for something?' 'Oh, just out for a wander, you know,' replied Nellie, her smile weakening slightly. The Constable, putting his foot in the door, continued: 'I hear there was a shipwreck illegally ransacked a couple of days ago and some of the treasure brought to our beach down there. You were seen leaving the beach with a basket. May I ask what was in it?'

'Oh, yes. Well, we collect interesting pebbles, you know. They look so lovely in water, keep their shine, you see.' Nellie was beginning to blush.

'Oh really, may I see?' said the Policeman, stepping into the hall. He saw Doris sitting on the edge of the sofa, looking very awkward, twisting her hands. Seeing the officer, she cried:

'Oh Nellie, is it about the treasure? I knew it was wrong, somehow, hiding them like that.'

'I think we had better get to the bottom of this, ladies,' said the Constable, taking out his notebook and pencil. 'Better let me see what you've found. It's all round the village about that ship, and we have the crew at the Station. They're for it, smuggling treasure in like that. And they knew some coins were lost, and you were seen coming up the cliff path with a basket. We put two and two together. You do realise that treasure found on beaches has to be declared, don't you? Beaches are Crown Property, that means they belong to the Queen. It's a criminal offence not to declare what you've found. I'm sorry, ladies, but I might have to take you down to the Station if you don't own up.'

Doris was on her feet. 'Oh my Lord! What have we done, Nellie? We'll have to own up now. I don't want to go to prison!'

Nellie sighed. 'All right, calm down, Doris. Dear, honest Doris. I thought it must be too good to last. Ah well, maybe we won't be rich after all. Come this way, Constable.' And she led him into her bedroom and showed him the contents of the caddy, which he took away with him in a plastic bag.

It was a couple of days later when someone in the shop told them a man who said he was a Policeman, and wore a uniform, had been asking about the two ladies seen on the beach, and Sam, who happened to be buying some sandwiches, in all innocence had given him their address. Nellie and Doris exchanged shocked glances, picked up their shopping and walked briskly home.

The following week, Nellie was in the greenhouse tying up her tomatoes, when she felt into her trouser pocket for some string. There was something else in there. It was hard and almost round, and she pulled it out - that silver doubloon. Smiling broadly to herself, she returned to the house.

Back in the privacy of her bedroom, she dropped it into her Mother's tea caddy, locked it up and put it back in its usual place on the window sill.

***

A CHRISTMAS POEM

Christmas is coming, it came, and it went;
And then I looked at the money I'd spent.
Where did it go? It can't be right
That the cash at the bank is so very light?
It was cheques for the children,
And flowers for a friend,
And stocking fillers without end.
And then there was food to fill the table
On Christmas morn; we were just about able
To eat it all up and stagger away
To have a lie down for the rest of the day.

It's over at last, the cards put away.
The tree's in its box till next Christmas Day.
We've eaten the leftovers, the birds had the rest,
We're back to normal, which feels much the best.
The good part was seeing the family again,
So it's not really wasted, not such a strain,
For all that effort for one special time,
We don't mind the money, we don't give a dime,
If everyone's happy and safe and well,
We shall do it again, I'm pleased to tell.

***

Diana Warmington

A LONG LONDON WEEKEND

It was a very early start – the 4.40 a.m. National Express coach to London Victoria. My own fault; I didn't want to go by train, as it turned out to be rather expensive, and I didn't want the later coach, because it arrived too late in the evening for me to meet with my daughters and get to the theatre in good time. So the early bus was the one. Taxied there by my dear husband, fully dressed – not in his dressing-gown, fortunately – and there were a few other shivering souls waiting at the coach stop on Bideford Quay to reassure us we were there on the right day at the right time. Waving goodbye through the tinted window, I settled back, duly belted up, for the five hour journey. I have never minded its length, as I like to watch both town and countryside as we travel along, and this time saw a watery dawn breaking as we approached the Tiverton turning. National Express visit all the small towns on the way to the M4, including Instow, Fremington, Barnstaple, South Molton, Wellington, South Petherton, Taunton, and Bridgwater, so there's plenty to see. In those early hours I could notice who was or was not awake between 5.00 and 7.00 a.m. - the occasional bathroom light on, or someone making tea in a kitchen became something to look out for.

It was a pleasant journey, with the trees in full bloom – cherry, both wild and cultivated, hawthorn, magnolia and apple in the gardens along the way. Being high up, one can see over the hedges into these gardens, and have a brief glimpse into people's lives, the back yards as well as the tidy front facade. Taunton wowed me with its hotel off the square, completely covered with climbing wisteria, a wonderful sight.

The coach remained half-full all the way until we reached Heathrow, where suitcase-burdened passengers struggled to find their tickets, and having had their luggage stowed away in the hold, sidled along the aisle to sink into the comfortable seats on the coach. We were off again, this time heading for Central London, and I just love to see the different architecture, dating from the early 20th century in the suburbs, to Edwardian and Victorian mansions as the coach approaches Chiswick and Hammersmith. On the right just after Hammersmith is a row of artists' houses; terraced houses, with steps up to a grand doorway, but on the upper floor, huge arched windows, masses of glass, and north facing to let in subdued light, with much terracotta decoration around every portal. I make sure I sit on the right side of the bus every time I go so as not to miss them.

The next excitement comes as we travel along the Embankment, the Thames on one side, with all the house and tourist boats lined up, and on the other side, enormous Victorian and Georgian homes, covered in wisteria, boasting pillars and plasterwork, and money. Then it's into the streets of London until the coach finds its tortuous way into the Coach Station. Time to descend, make my way to the Tube – find my Oyster card, and rattle my way to Holloway Road.

My daughter lives in a leafy avenue of Victorian terraced apartments, the kind with a flight of steps up to a huge front door, a black and white tiled entrance hall, and winding staircase up to the first and second floors. The flats stand at either side of the central stairway, and consist of a large drawing room overlooking the street, two bedrooms, a bathroom and a kitchen-diner. All have high ceilings and windows requiring long curtains. She uses the front room as her bedroom (which she gave to me during my stay) and the diner as her sitting-room, as it gets all the sunshine and overlooks a small garden, and is a more pleasant room in which to relax.

We were joined by my eldest daughter who had arrived from Bournemouth, and we walked to a small Italian restaurant nearby for our evening meal, family owned, friendly and fun. As we finished our meal, the proprietor proudly brought along a tray of Italian liqueur, smooth and sweet, on the house. We did manage to say thank you in Italian, which made him laugh.

Walking back to the flat, we crossed the ever-busy Holloway Road, always using the pedestrian crossings, traffic is fast, no one seems to slow down for anything, let alone people walking.

Our sleeping arrangements favoured me in my matriarchal status, as I was given the double bed, my daughters making the best of a floor mattress and the sofa, my grandson happily in his top bunk. But we all slept pretty well, and prepared ourselves for the day ahead. Ros, my youngest, decided we should see something she had come across by chance, taking a wrong turn on her way home to Islington from the Oasis Nature Garden in Stockwell. She had noticed a woodland beside the road, turned into the car park and wandered through the trees. She suddenly came upon an amazing structure, a wooden pergola, raised on brick arches, stretching along a garden of shrubs and flowers. At the end, the pergola continued at a right angle, crossed the garden on a bridge, where a tower room had been built, and she realised there was much more beyond. She took us to this place in the Clapham area, I have yet to find it on the map, and we walked through the forest together, the dappled sunlight filtering through the canopy of tall trees, the ground bare of vegetation .

And then we saw what she had seen – this stunning folly, built in the Italian style, all pillars and pilasters, a walkway for the rich and idle to while away their sunny afternoons, weekend party guests strolling along, conversation and drinks flowing. Perhaps a romance would flourish in such a setting, the raised pathway led to some intimate corners, and wound its way far from the house, well out of sight of parental eyes.   It turned out that the house behind the pergola had been built by Lord Lever, the Persil and soap magnate, later Lord Leverhulme, and dated back to Edwardian times, its architecture palatial, with a long veranda, a double stairway, such a one sees at stately homes, leading to terraced gardens and a lily pond.

But that wasn't all, a short walk away lay another garden, surrounded by beautiful trees, azalias and rhododendrons, well-cut lawns, and tidy flower beds. The whole area was a curiosity, an antique treasure that had been neglected for some years, but someone had realised that it was very special, and much had been done to restore it to its original beauty and status as a work of art. We were all so happy to have been there. I met a woman walking along one of the paths, and she said she had lived in this area for some time before discovering this hidden treasure, she just never knew it was there. Now she visited it regularly, couldn't keep away.

Follow that! We agreed it had been a wonderful morning, and driving back through the suburbs and then into the City, we realised what a paradise that pergola must be for Londoners, just to get away from their frantic lifestyle. London actually does have a lot of parks for that very reason, undoubtedly. We dropped off my eldest daughter near to Euston, as she had to get back to Bournemouth, and we wound our way back to Islington.

I then got myself ready for the purpose of my visit – to attend the Fitness League Festival in the Albert Hall, where about 3000 members were assembled, some to perform routines, and some, like me, just to watch them at it. Ladies of all ages, from teens to nineties, had come from all over the world to perform or just be there. We watched as women from South Africa danced around a huge drum; New Zealanders danced their routine with ribbons, and a group of Fitness League tutors showed off with a routine using coloured umbrellas. It was an event full of fun, as well as admiration for the dancing, all with the purpose of keeping women subtle, strong, and confident about balance and health, both physical and mental, into old age. The Fitness League teaches women about anatomy, internal and external, we often learn why we get aches and pains, and what to do about them. The Bagot-Stack exercises began in the 1930s, when women in offices were given a short routine to keep them fit while enduring a sedentary job, and it blossomed into a world-wide enterprise, with village and town halls taken over for day and evening classes. I joined in my 30s, had to leave while working, but returned at the age of 65 and immediately felt stronger.

The Albert Hall is a magnificent building, with corridors encircling the central arena, and its seating arrangements rise from almost ground level to the 'gods' near the roof. Off the corridors are endless rooms, for meetings, changing clothes, cafés and toilets. From the outside it is as good as the Taj Mahal, with its tiers of windows rising up towards the dome. Opposite is the Albert Memorial, a golden Albert surrounded by sculptures in white marble, rising above us like a god.

After another night with my daughter and her son, I took the tube to Putney, and spent a happy few hours with an old school friend who has a flat beside the Thames; she is a member of the Hurlingham Club, just along the road, and we had lunch on the terrace – a very long wait for it, too, as there were so many other members attracted by the glorious weather on that sunny Sunday.

Leaving her in the early afternoon, I made my way to another part of Islington, off Roseberry Avenue, where my middle daughter lives with her partner. In the evening, we strolled along to a small square where there were two restaurants – one French, the other, Italian. We chose the French one, and soon realised that it was not just the food that was French, but the owner and waiters were the genuine article. Needless to say, the food was very good; I had salmon in a wonderful dressing, then a chicken dish quite out of this world, and some excellent wine.

I slept well in my daughter's flat, in the spare room where all the bicycle parts are kept – her partner makes bikes, racing bikes, and keeps a lot of spares at home, and in a 4th floor flat, they have to be kept somewhere!

Next day, my daughter and I went to the Wallace Collection off Manchester Square, where I was particularly interested to see the Reynolds collection. The Wallace is best known for 'The Laughing Cavalier' by Frans Hals, and when you find it, it's surprising how small it is compared with some of the epic tales depicted by other artists in that room. The Reynolds Collection was a great pleasure; his portraits of beautiful women and children are especially fine, and he was much in demand for most of his life. He died in 1792 aged 69. Galleries can be tiring, and luckily they all have seating where one can rest and take in the enormity of the collection. In the end, one tends to keep walking through, as there are just too many paintings to study in detail. But the Reynolds was worth taking time over.

That evening, we chose the Italian restaurant, and were squeezed into the back room facing the bar and kitchen door, so got very friendly with the Italian staff – again, the genuine article. The food here was also good, and the extras, bread and olives standard on each table, and the Spritzer-type wine, very red and sparkly, was something I could get used to. Both restaurants, French and Italian, were entertaining, and when one considers how hard the staff work, day after day, serving with a smile to a crowded restaurant, in the middle of London, I appreciated the welcome they tirelessly – or so it seems – give to their customers. No wonder they were busy, people just keep coming back. I certainly would.

Next day I had to say goodbye to my daughter, take the tube to Victoria Coach Station, climb aboard No. 502 to Westward Ho! and enjoy a relaxing ride home. At Heathrow, a teenager came and sat beside me, her father on the opposite side of the aisle. After a lot of chat, she got out her iPad and out of the corner of my eye, on the screen, I could see Jeremy Paxman interviewing someone, live or recorded, I knew not which, she was listening through earphones. Then she got out her mobile and scrolled away for a while, then plugged her ears into that, and listened to music, I guess. She also had a notebook and did some revision, so I guessed exams weren't far off. She must have had access to just about all the social media going, and I felt very old-fashioned when I got out my antique mobile to call my husband to say I was nearing Bideford!

He met me on the Quay, and I was home and eating the supper he had prepared – well, thawed out from the freezer – by 7.00, after a very memorable and enjoyable long weekend in London.

***

THE JOURNEY

He has been walking for nineteen days, the record he writes in the road atlas tells him so. Last night he wrote, 'Day 19, Minehead to Porlock.' It was late June when he left Birmingham so it must be well into July now.

He closes the map and from his vantage point stares out at the vast, silent sea bounded only by the hazy outline of Wales on the horizon. It is the first time on his journey that he has been able to look at his surroundings without the fear of being observed. Below and to his right is the long, grey, pebbly beach, and beyond Porlock Weir itself, with its row of houses beside the water, and a hotel, its white walls shining in the sun. A few chairs and tables were set outside with several customers enjoying a drink. The glare from a shop window flashed against his eyes, and he noticed a few children playing with a dog in the road. Beyond, another grey building which looked like a café, led to a slender bridge with railings, and he could see the channel where the sea washed through, making an inner harbour, a safe anchorage for a few yachts. The wide harbour wall stretched further out, with fishermen's pots stacked up beside a large, hip-roofed, white painted building, standing alone. To the north, stretching well out into the sea, a long line of raised shingle was lapped by the incoming tide.

He took all this in as he rested on a grassy slope at the side of the steep hill which descended from the high cliffs. He felt the warmth of the sun on his back, almost too hot on his neck. He realised it was some time since he last ate, just a drink of water, a sandwich and a chocolate bar he had bought at a wayside garage after leaving Minehead. He had been tempted to stop off at the Blue Ball at the top of the long hill, but wanted to get to Porlock before dusk, and he knew he would have stayed too long in the pub, and probably drunk more alcohol than was good for him. Rising, he picked up his rucksack, and taking out his camera, took a few shots of the village below. Colours were vivid, the sea and sky were blue, and Wales was clearer this time. He checked the result, and was happy to have captured such a wonderful scene.

He set off down the rest of that long hill, and eventually walked along beside the hotel, the children playing, and went into the small café, which already held two families and an elderly couple. There was only one table left by the wall, and he squeezed himself into a metal chair. A girl with neat black hair, a pleasant smile and a smart apron approached him, and he asked for a menu. It was quite impressive, and he chose a baked potato and salad, tea and a cake. He was really hungry, and knew he must eat well, as he didn't know when his next meal would be.

The girl disappeared into the depths of the café, and he was left to look around. This café was obviously an outlet for local artists, and the walls held watercolours and oils of the local landscape. Most were quite good, and if he hadn't been travelling, he might well have purchased one of them, but it was out of the question, considering his situation. The less luggage the better.

He was glad to be off his feet for a while, and stayed in the café for some time after eating, enjoying his cup of tea. His toes hurt, and he longed to take off his shoes, but this was not the place. He must move on. Having paid for his repast, he thanked the girl and set off for the narrow bridge over the entrance to the inner harbour. The tide had turned. The waves were a little stronger now, reaching further in, and he stood for a moment on the bridge, watching the water as it was pulled to and fro beneath him. He was mesmerised by it, but was shaken out of his reverie by the shrill voices of children, as they dashed past him with their dog. Their happy faces would normally make anyone smile, but for him it caused a pang of pain, and his eyes filled with tears. He watched them running along the spit of pebbles that ran out to sea, and was suddenly concerned that they might slip and fall on the uneven surface.

But they almost seemed to dance along, he needn't have worried. The dog splashed in the surf, and the children skimmed stones to make them bounce.

He found a place to sit, and took off his walking shoes. They were heavy, and he heaved a sigh of relief to be without them. Socks came off rather stickily, and at last he felt the coolness of the stone flags under his feet, and he got up and walked around to make it last. Looking across at the water, he decided he needed to wash his tired feet, and picking up his belongings, he walked past the white house, and on towards the pebbled beach and the cool, cool, salty sea. The rounded stones proved difficult to walk on; he realised he wasn't as nimble as the children, and knew his balance wasn't as good as theirs. He managed to get near the water in the end, and, sitting down on one of the larger stones, stretched out his sore toes to touch the waves. Gently they lapped and soothed the aching, and although refreshingly cold, they brought him a sense of peace. But it was short-lived. Looking at the horizon, he looked back on his journey; he had created a space between himself and his pursuers, so far now that he almost felt safe. No one knew him in this corner of the South West, he could walk for miles without anyone looking twice at a lone walker. Hundreds of people hiked and camped in this holiday area, so what's new?

Looking at his map again, he saw the road he must take to get even further south, and onto moorland. There seemed to be a coastal path that ran along the cliffs, which he must make for before it got dark. He took out a handkerchief to dry his feet, and, with difficulty, managed to get his socks and shoes on again. Shakily, he staggered back across the pebbles to the pathway, crossed the bridge, and walked past the café and hotel. As he passed, someone called a hello, and waved to him, and he froze, transfixed with fear, who was it? Turning furtively to look at the caller, he realised it was just a man, a stranger, who had been sitting outside and had seen him pass by earlier. He managed a weak wave of the hand, and walked on. His heart was beating far too fast, sweat started on his forehead, and his legs turned to jelly. Would it always be like this?

Every time someone looked at him for more than a second, would he panic? He groaned. His pack seemed heavier than ever, and his feet hurt again. He could see a steep hill ahead of him. Porlock is at sea-level with high cliffs on both sides. He would have to climb whichever way he chose to go, whether on the road or up the path to the Valley of Rocks. He was so tired, he just wanted to lie down somewhere and sleep, for a long, long time.

What he had done, back home in Birmingham, was obviously wrong. In desperate need of money through gambling and drinking, he had changed a few digits on the firm's ledger and made the surplus cash go directly into his own account. All seemed well for a few weeks. No one had noticed, but one or two insinuations about errors in the accounts made him realise the game was up. He had drawn out the money straight away and left at night, wrote a brief note for his son, and just walked and walked until he was out in the suburbs. He slept where he could, usually at a wayside lodge, where no questions were asked. He paid in cash so there was no trace of his cards, and had begun to enjoy his freedom, the open road – or rather, the open back-road – until he reached the sea.

Looking again at the horizon, he wondered what the future held for him. Always on the run, until the cash ran out. What then? He would have no friends, as they would want to know his background, and once lies have started, they are difficult to maintain. And what about his son? That was the worst part; what must the boy be thinking of a father who just walked off and left him alone, with no idea of when he would return. How could he do such a thing and have no conscience? In the middle of the road, he stopped, turned round and made his way back to the hotel. Entering the foyer, he stepped up to the Reception desk.

'Can I help you sir,' asked the young man cheerfully. 'Yes, please. May I use your phone?'

***

THE LAKE

There was definitely someone standing alone on the bank on the other side of the lake. Alone myself, I glanced across as I walked along the footpath towards the wood. I didn't like to look face on to this person, in case they wanted not to be noticed, but out of the corner of my eye, I could see dark clothing on the body, but the arms hanging at her sides, and her legs below the knee were whiter, as if bare. The face and neck also showed pale, and the hair was dark. There was enough evening light for me to pick out this person, this woman, as she stood there, staring across – was it at me? I hoped not, it wasn't anyone I recognised, and I hurried on, but the hairs on my arms tingled, and a feeling of unease coming over me. If she had moved, walked along the path, swinging her arms, looking as if she was out for a walk, I wouldn't have given her another thought, but to be just standing there, motionless, watching me – that wasn't right. I decided not to look back as I walked on, quickening my pace a little, so as to get nearer my goal, the end of the lake where it tapered into a stream, and ran downhill in little waterfalls to join the river half a mile away.

I often took this route in the late afternoon, to walk off the day's work, clear my head of all the decisions, the targets to be reached, the directives from head-office, and grumbles from the staff. The walk usually refreshed me, and helped me to sort out a few of those problems, but this time I couldn't get that figure across the lake out of my mind, and as I reached the little bridge over the stream, I looked again to where she was. Or had been. There was no one there now, no sign of her, and I began to wonder if she had gone back, or whether she had followed my direction and was closer to me. What if she was there, behind the trees, watching me again? I strained my eyes and ears, in case I could pick out movement on that side of the lake. But I was puzzled. Thinking about it, I realised that there wasn't actually any access to that side of the lake, only the path I took from the main road above. One would have to pass through a tangle of brambles and rough ground to get to where she was, so how did she get there without my seeing her somewhere along my way?

I must calm down.

Perhaps I had imagined her, and looking around, I could see no one. But I was certain I had seen someone. In my mind's eye, I recalled the dark hair, the bare limbs, the white face. I didn't believe in ghosts, but shivered at the thought. Enough! I really ought to turn back and go home; the sun had gone down, leaving pink and grey streaks in the sky, and the gaps between the trees were darker now and rather threatening. Turning back from the bridge, I started to return to the road. And there she was, standing between me and the end of the footpath. She was still a distance away, black and white in the dusky light, motionless, watching. I stopped, trapped, unable to progress, fearful and confused. Panicking, I looked around to see if there was another route to get away from this awful place, but the shrubby trees along the path were too close together, and the dark water of the lake beside me gave no comfort. I had no alternative, if I was to get home at all that evening, but to walk slowly towards her. I took some deep breaths to give myself courage, and called out to her, but there was no reply, just that blank stare which seemed to penetrate my soul. I moved forward, and as I did so, so she moved away from me, somehow drifting backwards without effort. I didn't seem to get any nearer to her. I tried walking faster, and the same thing happened, and this continued until we were nearer the end of the path, where it turned upwards towards the road. And at that bend in the path, she disappeared.

I desperately wanted to see her again, to find out where she had gone, and hurried towards the place where I last saw her. Nothing. Not a sign of anyone, I was completely alone. I realised I was shivering, partly due to the coolness that had descended since I set out, and partly due to the eerie feelings that had haunted me - why did I use the word 'haunt'? Perhaps I had seen a ghost. Nonsense. But what? Home called, and I wasted no more time getting there.

A few weeks later, picking up my local newspaper as it fell from the letterbox, I noticed a side-heading on the front page. It seemed that a woman had committed suicide by walking into a lake, the very one where I had taken my walk. Reading on, I saw that she must have done this in the early morning of my strange sighting; but there was more – she was named. I knew that name. She and I had been at school together, were close friends as teenagers, but had grown apart, gone our own ways and lost contact. I had not recognised her across the water, but she had recognised me. Tears filled my eyes as I realised it was me she was calling to, silently, on that fateful evening.

***

THE PARK

I'm waiting. Always waiting. Sitting here, in the Park, beside the children's play area, waiting for what? A familiar face, figure, way of walking, that particular coat and hat, that smile? I don't think it will be today. It was a long time ago that we met, so perhaps she won't recognise me now anyway. But she always came here with her children, and I with mine, and we watched them climb and slide, and run and hide, and shout and laugh until it was time to go home. It always seemed to be sunny then, blinking against the glare, shading one's eyes, just making sure the children were safe, not falling, not pushing, not hurting, just happy to be together having fun. No, it won't be today, perhaps tomorrow she might come this way, to remember, like me.

So I shall sit here in the autumn sunshine, watching other people's children running and skipping, and swinging far too high. One boy calls to his mother to watch me, watch me, while I dare to get to the top of the climbing frame! The small figure, still in his green and grey school uniform, grabs the struts of the frame, and shins up as fast as a monkey to the very top. A cheer goes up as the feat is achieved, the child waving from on high, laughing, balancing, and clinging to the poles with tight little fists. He stays there a while, relishing his courage, staring around him to see if the other boys have noticed. He calls again until one or two look up, but they turn away and carry on kicking their ball.

Mother calls him to come down – he frowns, and shrugs, slightly embarrassed, but he obeys. I watch as he slowly descends, fearfully placing one foot after another, looking up and then down, hand over hand until the last rung, when that monkey reappears and he jumps and lands with a shout and a laugh.

It's getting late. The sun has gone in, and I feel the cold of early evening. The families have gone, leaving traces of their passing, the swings still gently describing an arc, diminishing by the minute. Litter blows around, paper and packets that held sweets and crisps, mixing with the leaves piling up along the edges of the path. The trees are almost bare now, no longer scarlet and gold, their lifeline scattered to the winds, leaving them naked and vulnerable. But stored within are new beginnings ready to burst forth in the Spring. Nothing is lost.

I get up to go. Not many people around now. A few lads in the distance are still kicking their ball around on the pitch next to the playground, and I hear their banter. A man walks his dog, stopping every few yards as the dog demands. He nods to me as he passes, and I acknowledge the brief contact. I walk towards the open gate. No hurry, it isn't dusk yet, when they come to lock it up. I'm not ready to go home yet. I will walk all the way, not use the bus this time, it will take longer to get there. If it's fine again tomorrow, I'll go and wait in the Park again, just in case she comes to find me there.

***

THE RIVER

A very high tide today, a 6.5. This tidal river flows into the Bristol Channel, one of the two fastest tides in the world – the other is in Canada – and when the moon is full, or the equinox is due, the river reaches its highest point. But now there is more water than ever. So much rain has fallen on fields and forests, and up river, near Beam Bridge, the flooding water is dashing over the weir, tearing around the next bend, washing its wooded banks, pulling at the trees, until they offer up their lowest branches, which break off and bob down towards the estuary, clogging against the bridges, piling up the debris. The ancient bridge stands firm; only a foot or two of its many arches left showing above the water level. The starlings, which perch each night inside those arches, fled early today, not to be caught out by the rising, threatening surge of water and litter.

And then, gradually, the tide recedes, as it always will. The banks shine with silver mud, and sea birds and water fowl descend to feed. A heron strides slowly in the shallows; a black-legged egret stalks elegantly nearby. Mallard arrive in groups, gliding silently together. Herring and black-headed gulls peck the mud, seeking out the lug worms that lie there, unaware of the predators above. Redshanks appear, running here and there, dipping their beaks to catch their prey.

It is a calm day, no wind, and the river slowly moves towards the sea, revealing more and more of its underbelly, until there is just one channel of deeper water, a few rippled sandbanks, and shallow pools. It is hard to imagine the immense depth of water only an hour or two ago. The birds fly up, disturbed by a man, bucket and trowel in hand, trudging across the mud to dig for lugworm bait. He leaves a trail of deep footprints, going out, digging, turning about, finally returning to firmer ground.

Sailing boats and dinghies sit tilted on the riverbed, their mooring ropes drooping, the orange buoys half submerged. Older craft lie deserted on the riverbank, their paint peeling, stained with mud below, lifted and swaying on the incoming tide, just twice a day, their only venture, trapped in time.

It is afternoon, and the wind rises, the tide has turned and the water creeps silently over the rippled sandbanks, lapping the shore with bubbling wavelets. The stranded boats begin to lift; the anchored ropes pull tight from the bow as they turn and stop. The troubled surface of the water is streaked with shimmering light, and all the time the river is moving forward with a power that cannot be halted, man has no control over it, and can only watch and wait and hope. But he knows he will be safe again, and that however high the tide, the river will always return to the sea from whence it came.

***

Elizabeth Fowler

A deep seated love of change and a fertile imagination has shaped Elizabeth's life from the very earliest days, of being required to tell her sisters stories when they were all small, to now finding fun and enjoyment in once more creating tales. The many and wonderfully diverse jobs she has done, from driving a mobile library through Cheshire, running a narrowboat business across the English canal system, commercial cooking to architecture while always close to the world of Devon farming which was her life for the first 45 years, this all now provides endless ideas and story lines. She honed her writing ability through short travel features for several different magazines and the short story is perfectly suited to her butterfly approach to life where a new venture is constantly ahead.

A MOST UNUSAL PENSION

I'd been digging for almost three hours and was beginning to get tired but it was such a perfect night, a clear almost full moon meant that I could work without any extra light secure in the knowledge that I was very unlikely to be seen. The previous two nights had not been so good and I had given up after a couple of hours when it started raining on the first night and heavy black clouds obscured the moon on the second evening, but I was quite sure I was in the right place and I would be staying in the cottage another few nights. Plenty of time to find it.

I had booked this week's holiday in the tiny remote cottage as a nostalgic trip back to boyhood and hoped to find the space to sort out my life. It was on the side of one of the remote Exmoor combes and quite enchanting with the stream tumbling along the bottom of the valley and glorious views away over the moor.

I'd come down with my parents to this isolated moorland cottage on holiday in the early 60s. It belonged to a distant cousin of my father and had been pretty primitive then. My town bred mother had hated it, so we never went back. It may still have been completely alone but now it certainly had all the comforts I could have wished for, with the added bonus of no mobile signal. Once again I could enjoy the peace and delight of exploring the natural world around me. Arriving on the first evening I had been rewarded with the sight of seven wonderful hinds grazing on the hill opposite.

Strolling down to the pub on the following evening for a hearty meat pie and a perfect pint of Exmoor Ale, I was listening idly to a group of local men talking about Reuben's funeral that afternoon, when one of them brought up the subject of old Reuben's mystery pension. Apparently Reuben had told everyone some 40 years before that he had found the cache of jewellery that was the last haul taken by Jeremiah Ford, the highwayman, before he was caught and hanged. Reuben had told everyone in the village that he had then reburied it out on the moor for safe keeping until he needed it for his old age. He said it was his insurance against the future. But now he had died suddenly, before apparently retrieving his unusual pension, or fully divulging where he had buried it.

My ears pricked up and I started to say, 'But I. . .'

They all turned to look at the stranger at the corner table and queried, 'but you what?'

'Oh um, but I've never heard that story, it sounds good.' No one needed asking again to repeat this local gem of a tale.

Reuben had come into the pub one evening back in about 1963 claiming to have found the jewellery that Jeremiah stole from Lady Fortesque as she was travelling back to London from North Devon. Reuben had even described the sapphire tiara that was apparently part of the collection. The highwayman had been caught soon afterwards and hauled off to Taunton jail, but had refused to divulge where he had cached the gems and went to the scaffold defiantly shouting that the nobs would never see their trinkets again.

Over the years since, when he had a belly full of cider, Reuben had let slip small bits of information as to where he had hidden the jewellery. Most of the local people had been out on the moor at one time or another looking for the mysterious haul. Many eventually decided that Reuben was not beyond pretending to let slip some small detail when he was in his cups as a useful way of making sure someone would buy him another pint. He always seemed to have a snippet to reveal, keeping the interest alive, and the cider flowing. When the locals eventually gave up he turned his attention to passing visitors. Still no one knew the truth of the matter and now Reuben himself was buried it would stay an unsolved mystery.

Walking back up the combe to the cottage late that evening I was transported back to 1964 when I had last stayed here. I had spent every waking moment out on the moor or in and out of the stream, talking to the few farmers I met and absorbing the simple beauty of a hard life lived in a glorious landscape. I learnt so much about the animals, trees and plants, it was the awakening of a lifelong passion that saw me leaving school to work in the world of conservation.

On our last night there I had been woken by the scream of a vixen, and very proud of myself for knowing what it was, had slipped quietly out of bed, dragged on some warm clothes and gone out into the night. The moon was moving fitfully in and out of the clouds and when it went dark for a moment I stopped and sat at the base of a stunted small tree as I could see nothing for the time being.

Things were rustling in the undergrowth around me and I was listening intently when a different noise caught my attention. Someone was quietly approaching the small dell where I was. I froze in part terror and part interest as the shape came into view and stopped just below me. I was hidden by the shadow cast by the little tree and the figure was obviously quite unaware of my presence.

Putting down a small bag he began to dig a hole, then dropped a few large stones into the bottom, put the bag on top, covered it with more stones, then soil and finally dragged the bracken back over it. He then silently left in the direction of the village.

Back in bed again I could not decide what to do next morning. I knew I would be in serious trouble with mother if I admitted going out alone at night. So at breakfast I tried to bring the subject up by asking what a farmer would bury out on the moor. Father informed me quite categorically that they buried their dead animals and this was not something to discuss in front of mother.

We left that morning and I had forgotten the night time incident. Surprisingly it had not resurfaced when I booked the cottage through a fancy holiday company or when I arrived. Maybe the cottage was so different that it did not jog my memory as it might otherwise have done. So, to hear that someone claimed to have been burying a casket when I had been down that summer brought it all vividly back to mind and I decided to try and find the cache myself as I was sure I had seen it buried.

I was certain the small stunted tree was the one I had hidden beneath on that night as a 10 year old, so it should have been easy to locate the burial place. I went back to the tree and decided to sit down and try to recreate what I would have seen as a boy. This is when I realised that I misjudged the position by standing to locate it. From low to the ground it was obvious that I had been digging too far over. Moving to a slight dip nearer the tree I started again. It seemed hardly any time before my spade hit an obstruction and I dug furiously around it before uncovering the rotting sacking covering a small chest.

Pulling the chest out from the stones that still covered it I sat back in awe. Turning it around I tried lifting the small catch and found to my surprise it was not locked. Holding my breath in suspense I open the chest and under the few small rocks it contained I found an ancient, rather tatty pension book. Incredulously I opened it and found written after the final withdrawal the words.

'Ha, fooled you here, but I have enjoyed the cider. See you in the pub.'

***

GARDEN SONG

Out into the garden the little boy sped,
With happy thoughts tumbling inside his small head.
The garden was sunny as he went to play.
With a promise to mother that he would not stray.

He launched himself off, out over the lawn.
A brave fighter pilot on an air raid at dawn.
He shot down those planes with fearsome rat-tat,
One was a robin, the other Dad's cat.

He counted the wood lice found under a slate,
And chased a small mouse that ran under the gate.
He found an old football, so kicked a great goal,
Then stamped a mound that was made by a mole.

Then down by the greenhouse a hole he did spy,
And fetched a sharp stick into it to pry.
The wasps did not like this and out they all came
Buzzing and furious to attack who's to blame.

Crying and frightened back home he then flew,
Where Mum had to deal with the wasps that came too.
Now cuddled and cared for, with his favourite toy,
The garden's too scary for a four year old boy.

***

Elizabeth Fowler

HOUND TROUBLE

The lurid yellow of a hi-viz jacket was moving slowly across the skyline as Philip waited for the clouds to drift towards the sun and give him the exact light he wanted for this photograph. Perfect, a very slight haze to the strong glare softened everything enough to create the atmosphere he was looking for. But that damned vivid yellow was now standing almost centre in his view. Pointless to take anything till it was gone.

So he sat and looked through what he had achieved that last hour while waiting for the right conditions. At this time of the morning he had hoped to be alone. After a short while the jacket disappeared into a small dip and Philip relaxed. This could just be the winning one. It had the perfect composition he had been looking for. So much could be done back on the computer with a photograph, but the essence had to be there to start with and he had a natural gift for framing a picture.

As everything came together and he steadied his camera to get a series of shots a large dog came bounding across the ground barking furiously at him, followed by the yellow jacket shouting ineffectively, 'Jason come here, Jason no, Jason come back.' Eventually the dog turned and followed its master. He made no attempt to apologise to Philip who was now seething with annoyance. But good photos of the sort he was trying to create need a steady hand and quiet concentration. Eventually he took the last photos and set off on his bike for home.

Downloading all the morning's work he started the slow job of selecting anything with potential. Coming to the final section, which had been thoroughly disturbed by the man and dog, he stopped in surprise. The one he had been taking when the dog appeared was truly dramatic. He must have turned slightly, still clicking, as the dog leapt towards him, for on the computer screen was a scene straight out of "The Hound of the Baskervilles". The background had blurred slightly and the sky was full of clouds, but the dog was in sharp focus, mouth wide and fangs bared.

Quickly going into his editing programme he darkened the sky, casting a heavy look across the photo, then with care he reddened the dog's eyes and the inside of its mouth, making the teeth into glaring white fangs. He had been photographing from a lying position and the dog was above his sight line. It was a magnificent fluke and produced something amazing.

Photography had been his passion since he was 14 when his grandmother gave him her professional camera. Now it went everywhere with him and he was gathering an impressive portfolio while taking photography as one of his subjects at sixth form college. The end of year two was in sight and the chance to put an entry into the big, end of course, competition.

He needed something to make his work stand out from the others in his year. If he could win the Brendan Trophy it might give him a start into a professional career. He sat looking at the photo wondering how he could turn what was a great shot into something outstanding. He had several excellent views of the cliff top area he had been shooting, but now the dog shot had taken over as the basis for something, he just did not yet know what.

An hour later he finished the preliminary work on the morning's photos, closed down his computer and went in search of food. Parents were at work and he was going back into college for the afternoon, so the photos were forgotten in the pressure of work building up to the final exams. It was so easy to get completely lost in photography and neglect the other subjects he was taking.

Walking home later an idea started to form, maybe he could create a series of photos gradually sliding from the beautiful landscape in sunshine, (he already had those shots) into a darker scene ending with the dog almost leaping out of the picture, that might just do it. But realistically he needed one or two of the dog in the distance approaching. How on earth was he to do that. He wondered if the man walked his dog there regularly, if so maybe he could get him to co-operate.

Returning to the cliff path two days later he met a woman walking her small poodle, not what he needed there, but talking to her he learnt that, yes, the owner of the large dog did walk most Mondays to Thursdays - she avoided those days as the dog was a blasted nuisance.

So on the next Monday morning with the light almost the same as the previous Thursday, Philip set out early to see if his luck was in. If things went to plan he could just make it back to college for the first lecture. He waited impatiently for an hour then the yellow jacket appeared. He was taking the same route, but this time he was walking with his arm around a companion. This shouldn't matter as they were too far off to be identified. You had to be so careful these days.

After a few moments the dog reached the right point and Philip jumped up, camera ready. As he hoped the dog saw him and came racing in his direction. A rapid series of frames and he was sure he had what was needed. No time to check, he was already a bit late for college.

At home that evening he got to work on the photos and the result was just as he wanted. A beautiful sunlit scene, becoming dark over 6 shots with the dog appearing and getting closer till the final enlargement when it positively leapt out of the photo. He also graded the size of the prints to give extra impact. Carefully inserted into a concertina fold of pockets he put it ready for submitting the next day.

In the final college week he learned that he had indeed won the Brendan Trophy, a very successful finish to his course. All the finalist's work was being displayed in the main hall and the College Governors were at an early private viewing. Philip, hovering by his stand, was trying to eavesdrop when a couple approached and he heard the woman say, 'Oh look John, that's our Jason, fancy our dog being in the winning photo.'

Philip moved nearer to introduce himself when she stood back from a close look at one of the middle photos and turned to her husband, 'And just WHO have you got your arms around?' Philip slid quickly behind the next board and decided it was a good moment to disappear.

HAVING A BABY

I'm going to have a baby
and don't know what to do.
Should I knit the little bootees
In pink or baby blue?

I'm going to be a mother,
There's such a lot to do.
Cot and clothes and nappies to buy,
It's all so very new.

I think I'm nearly ready,
My doctor says that's true.
Done the classes and read the books,
My! how the months just flew.

Having my first little baby
Might just be the family glue.
Leant over the moses basket,
Oh! How my mother will coo.

Soon going to have my baby,
Still don't know what to do.
Just muddle along with a bit of help,
I reckon I might get through.

SILVER FOX

The wind shrieked a cold gale as Henrietta stepped regally out of the car with the briefest of acknowledgements to the chauffeur who had run to open the door. Wrapped in a luxurious fur-trimmed coat she swept into the warm, brightly lit foyer. Her husband, in full dress uniform, scarcely managed to keep up with her as they went in for the regimental dinner commemorating the end of the war 10 years before. He was used by now to her delusions of grandeur and insistence on the best of everything and had retreated more and more into the company of his army comrades where he was welcome as a fine soldier.

Following Henrietta into the long dining hall he heard her demand attention and an escort to her place; pity the poor batman who would be serving her. To his delight James was seated separately, with the other senior officers. The meal was excellent, as were the speeches. There were moving tributes to the members of the regiment lost during the war and a special memorial to General Eaves who died that year in Northern Canada. He had played an heroic part in the Africa campaign and his decision to leave after the war and disappear into the far North was much regretted by his fellow officers and the men he led.

At the end of an enjoyable evening James went back to Henrietta's side to escort her out. They followed Major Eaves, General Eaves' young nephew, and his pretty wife, into the foyer where adjutants were hurriedly retrieving coats for the guests.

Accepting hers, Henrietta turned to say an imperious 'goodnight' to the Eaves just as Mrs Eaves put on her coat, a glorious silver fox fur. Henrietta's face turned white with annoyance, she rounded on James and with a pinched mouth spat out, 'Where on earth did she get *that*? Not on her husband's salary I'm sure. If he can afford it you must get one for me.'

Resigned to the inevitable barrage of requests that would fill the days till Henrietta got what she wanted, James called the next day on the Eaves. Rebecca was on her own and despite his gentle requests refused to say where the coat had come from, insisting that only her husband had that information. It did appear somewhat strange, as if there was a mystery here. She even seemed to regret having worn it.

As soon as an opportunity presented itself James found a quiet moment to talk to David Eaves. Explaining rather sheepishly that his wife thought the coat beautiful and would like something similar, James asked where it had come from.

This brokered an embarrassed silence before David explained that he really should never have had it. It had come back with him from France early in the war and had lain unused for the past years. James' reaction was that many soldiers had brought bits back with them, but a silver fox fur, that was really different and could he please hear the story. It truly would go no further.

David seemed almost relieved to share the story with someone as he recounted how he had been part of the army rescued from Dunkirk. The last billet he and his men found while the Germans were rapidly overrunning the area was above a furrier and jeweller. The shop's stock was bound to end up in Germany so the feeling of the men was why should they not liberate some. It was wrong, yes, but they excused themselves.

Reaching the beach they joined the long lines of soldiers wading into the sea while being strafed by German planes. He lost touch with most of his men in the chaos and carnage but managed to reach one of the small boats and was eventually brought back. When the regiment was together again in England the matter of 'souvenirs' was never mentioned and he had given the coat to Rebecca. After such a long time they thought it reasonable for her to start enjoying the coat. The weather had certainly been cold enough to justify wearing it.

Now it had been noticed, what on earth was he to do? He needed a properly convincing story of its provenance. They sat and discussed the problem until an idea came to James, one that would also help him avoid any notion of being expected to produce a similar coat.

When David's uncle General Eaves died in the Alaskan North of Canada, what had happened to his possessions? he had asked. Maybe the coat had been sent back to England with the rest of his things, no one would query that, and there was no way another such coat could be found in England. So two problems solved with one simple story.

***

THE SOUND OF AUTUMN

The sun was warm on his face as he sat by the river on his favourite seat where he regularly stopped and enjoyed the passing seasons. It was now late autumn, still warm and gentle, but he could smell the nip of winter in the air. Not too long before he would be bundled up in all his thickest winter clothes enjoying the sharp tang of frost and perhaps hearing the squeak of ice formed at the edge of the river.

'Afternoon Joe,' a familiar voice greeted him as the newcomer sat down on the bench. 'Don't think I've ever seen the trees looking so lovely as they do this year. That beech is an amazing burst of colour, even the oaks are colouring up now. Just look at that one, a glorious yellow on all the upper leaves, yet still fresh and green below, quite lovely. Wish I could paint it all, hold all that natural beauty in something I had created, that would make me proud.'

'Shift up Charles, make room for one more, you pontificating old bore.' Fred didn't hold with all that poetic nonsense and producing a large thermos from a battered sports bag poured cups of coffee for the three of them.

'Brilliant game that was last night, imagine you heard it all from your flat Joe. Great now that we have the lights, it looked good last night, brilliant lit up pitch and all the light reflecting off the mist that was coming down. Mind you that ref could do with glasses, reckon the fog was thick round him, right pathetic decisions he made, still we won and it was a great game. You were a good fly-half in your day Joe weren't you - ever go onto the ground now?'

'Oh! I wander across there when there's no game on, love to hear the oystercatchers and gulls, not happy when a dog chases them, but my stick comes in handy. The ground has felt good this season, just enough rain to keep it going but not churned up mud all the time, nice springy turf to walk on.'

They gossiped on for a while longer till Charles and Fred said cheerio and moved on. Joe sat enjoying the warmth and peace till that was shattered by the noisy arrival of a skate board. With a well practised clunk-bang Andy expertly jumped the kerb and brought his board to a stylish stop by the bench.

'Hello Andy, you been wasting your time at the board park again?'

Andy laughed, he knew Joe was teasing. 'Yes, but it was quite something this morning. All the leaves have blown into the park and they are so dry this year it was like skating through cornflakes.'

'Know just what you mean, I've always loved that crunchy sound, walking through the fallen leaves. You been taking any more photos recently?'

'Yes I have and I hope I got a really unusual one just now. Ben was at the park doing some flash runs and turns, so I was shooting him quite a bit and as he came down the big curl he twisted over in a sharp turn and all the leaves sprayed out behind him. It looked way out so I'm hoping I've got it. Just going back home to see what they look like on my computer.'

'Sounds like you could have something there, hope it works out well when you download them, never can be quite sure on the small camera screen.'

Andy moved off and the rumble of his board faded away. Joe liked talking to people but the peace here was special. He sat adjusting to it and the sounds of the natural world started to register. A small rustling behind the bench caught his attention, a bird? No not that, a small vole probably, hunting for it's dinner in the undergrowth. He could hear the ducks on the water and in the distance the plaintive cry of a curlew, autumn brought so many more birds to feed here in the estuary. He could often pick out up to a dozen different species. This morning there was a wren singing its heart out on a nearby bush. 'How did such a tiny bird manage all that sound,' he mused.

The Sound of Autumn

'Hello Mr Joe.' At the sound of a small voice he turned, 'Why hello Sally, what are you doing here this morning?'

'Mummy and I are walking to Aunty Jane and I've found something special. Actually I found three but one was broken so I have two now. They are so lovely and shiny and smooth, would you like to feel one.'

'Oh a conker, they do feel so nice, as you say all smooth and silky. What are you going to do with them?'

'I might give one to Peter when we get there, but I might keep them and put them on my bedroom table with my pretty shells. I think mummy wants to go now, are you going home Mr Joe, would you like me to take you?'

'That would be very nice, thank you Sally.' Joe reached down, picked up his white stick and taking Sally's hand they set off together.

***

THE READING BREAK

'What are you reading?'
'H'mm.'
'Never did learn to read, moved from school to school, always in trouble. It must be nice to read. Is that good?'
'Mmm.'
'Just forget about everything and have a good story. That was the only thing I really liked at school when I was small, the teacher reading a story. Never could do sums, everything just looked a jumble, got shouted at for that. Sums teacher hated me, so did the art teacher, always making a mess I was, couldn't help it somehow. Read a lot do you?'
'Mmm.'
'Couldn't wait to leave school, mind you I wasn't really there anyway, down the park playing footie. Reckon I could have been good at football if I'd stuck at it, quick I was, really fast down the line, got past the other boys easy. One of the dads came down to help us one winter, that was great, really got the game going, then he left and no one else cared. School played rugby, didn't like that, and tennis that was worse, always did well running, fast see. You ever play footie?'
'Hmm.'
'Came down here with mum when dad got banged up for a house job that went wrong. Saw him a couple of times in Wandsworth, never after he came out, that was OK, all he ever did before was shout at me. You ever read crime books?'
'Hmm.'
'I like those films on telly, there's a great big telly at the shelter but I never get to choose what's on, it's always Crossroads and Eastenders, don't like them. Used to like that policeman, what was he called? Drove an old car and drank a lot. That was good, did you like that?'

'Mmm.'

'I've only been down the shelter for a couple of months, had a job at the minimarket till it closed down cause that bloody great Tesco opened in Belle Vue. Had a room in Market Street, that was OK, but without a job couldn't pay the rent. You been doing this job long?'

'Hmm.'

'I'd like a job like yours, out in the open getting on with it, people to talk to. Think I'll ask the job centre woman if there's one going. What do you think?'

'Mmm.'

'It would be nice to read. Don't think you're listening to a word I'm saying.'

'Look will you shut up for a minute if I promise to teach you to read?'

***

THROUGH A BROKEN WINDOW

Sue cut down Irsha Street on her hurried way home from work and glanced through the broken window of number 13 as she ran past. What she saw stopped her in her tracks and she turned back, but the dirty room inside was empty. She can't have been mistaken, there had been someone there staring out through the glass. Sue felt a shiver run down her spine and walked quickly away, suddenly anxious to be at home.

Her mum had arrived home just before her and the kettle was already on. Greeting her daughter she asked how the day had been. 'OK,' Sue responded, 'but there was something odd on my way home.' And she described what she had seen.

'Oh, just a trick of the light I expect,' her ever so sensible headmistress mother said and carried her mug of tea upstairs to change out of her working clothes. Can it have been just that? 'A trick of the light,' thought Sue, but she was quite certain she had seen someone and the encounter left her shaken. This feeling of foreboding, of something wrong, she could not explain and through the ordinary evening at home it hung like a heavy presence over her.

The following evening Sue was undecided whether to walk home through Irsha Street again: half of her wanted to prove that there was nothing odd, the other half was almost frightened. Telling herself to stop being silly she walked purposefully past number 13. The bare room was quite empty, 'There you are,' she admonished herself, 'Nothing.' Stepping back to look properly at the front of the shabby house a faint gleam of flickering lamplight seemed to come from the room above. Was someone in the ruined house after all? Maybe, but nothing to do with her, so forget it.

That was easier said than done and on Saturday morning Sue found herself drawn back to Irsha Street. She peered in through the same window and in the shadowy room she could make out dusty footprints on the floor. Unable to leave it alone she tried the front door and found that it swung open easily, someone must have oiled the hinges very recently.

Entering the house her footsteps echoed gloomily back at her and she stopped, worried by what she was doing. She really should just leave. In the ensuing silence she made out a slight, muffled humming sound, as if a person was humming, but not a tune. Intrigued, she tried follow the sound which she believed was coming from upstairs.

The top of the stairs led straight into a draughty, empty bedroom with a door leading off it. No sign of what might have created the light she had seen. Following what she thought was the sound she crossed the room, through the opposite door and into another bedroom, but this one was being used. A table had the remains of a meal with plenty of empty bottles and a small bed stood against the wall, a grubby blanket on it.

A feeling of heavy menace lay over the shabby little room, but the humming was inaudible up here. So Sue cautiously made her way back down the narrow stairs, listening intently. The sound was coming from beneath her. Back in the dark, narrow hall she eased round the foot of the stairs and felt a door in front of her.

The noise she was hearing was urgent and louder now. It definitely came from behind this door, but it was locked. Running her hand down the side of it she felt a large bolt that was shot across the door. Sliding it back she pushed the door open and recoiled in shock. Curled up in a corner of what was a small back kitchen, half-hidden by a solid table was a pitiful teenage girl, with a band of tape across her mouth, tied securely to the old iron range that filled the small fireplace. The awful scene was lit by gloomy light filtering from a high window.

Sue rushed across and two terrified eyes looked up at her as she gently pulled the tape from the girl's face.

'He's coming back,' the girl sobbed. 'He'll find you.' Quickly Sue asked who was coming back and why was the girl there and heard a dreadful tale of how the girl's uncle had brought her here because she had refused his advances and made it clear she would have nothing to do with him.

Sue realised she had to get the girl out of there fast, but it was already too late as they heard the sound of the outer door opening and a brute of a man appeared in the kitchen doorway. 'Someone interfering are they?' he said quietly with heavy menace. 'Well you'd better stay a while, I think. Don't go away while I fetch a nice bit of rope.' Saying which he shut and bolted the door and they heard him go up the stairs.

With only moments before he was likely to return Sue had to do something fast. Dragging the kitchen table across to the door she wedged it hard up under the door handle, blessing the fact that it was a lever handle. But that would only hold for a short while. Next she fished the little picnic knife out of her bag, part of a Swiss army knife. The birthday present she had pleaded for aged 12, suddenly made a lot of sense and using it she cut the rope tying the girl.

How to get out? The tiny high window was their only hope. Using a heavy pan she found on the floor by the range she started bashing at the window. Thank goodness the wood was old and starting to rot. But now the girl's uncle was back and trying to force open the door. Suddenly the wooden window frame broke and Sue pushed the girl up through the narrow opening, then struggled to get herself through. The girl had dropped into a small yard and turned to grab Sue's arm and help pull her through just as the man broke in and dived at Sue's foot. A hefty kick and Sue was free, though now they were caught in a yard with solid walls and a stout door.

They both started shouting loudly for help. As the door led to a back alleyway their cries quickly brought neighbours from the houses on the other side. It developed into pandemonium as questions were shouted back and forth over the wall. Then someone reappeared with a heavy hammer and the door was soon opened. Sue and the girl fell out into the waiting arms of a group of extremely worried people and they were led across into a warm kitchen, the girl clinging to Sue and trying to thank her through the tears and sobs of relief that engulfed her. Then while the police were summoned they were given a welcome cup of tea.

***

TOYS AND BOYS

Mervin slicked back his hair and sauntered into the great hanger that housed ranks and ranks of shelved toys. 34 aisles of shelves, six high, packed with every plastic toy available. He was working in Toys R Us for the pre-Christmas month and hoping to get some games for his X-box. The pay was not much but the staff discount was good and he might be able to lift something.

He'd been lucky last weekend and spent the days skulking around at the back of the store where the games were displayed. There had been two others also covering that section so he had been able to avoid doing any work and he was looking forward to more of the same this weekend.

It was 10 minutes to nine, Saturday morning, and all the sales staff were gathered waiting for the manager to give them their orders for the day. Mervin moved until he was behind Cheryl and started poking her in the back and muttering, 'Who's going to play with dollies today? Who's going to have tea parties with the little girlies?' She kicked him expertly in the shin with her heel and he stepped back glowering.

When his name was called he was told to follow Janice to aisle 14 where he was to work for the day. Janice was one of the senior sales staff and a pretty sharp-tongued woman, a basic necessity to work with the staff she had. Mervin had kept well out of her way last week. Now he was going to have to work under her. Not good, he decided. He then discovered to his horror that aisle 14 carried the huge display of Silvania Dolls and Sets; the My Little Ponies, even Barbie Dolls and he would be working with that spotty-faced Marlene. How would he ever face the gang if they found out?

Janice marched the two of them down the lines of toys pointing out where special items were displayed, giving them instructions on how to behave and reminding them that good sales figures were all that would keep them employed. She put Marlene to cover aisle 15 and Mervin on aisle 14. Once out of her sight, at the end of the row, he hitched his jeans down to the regulation low hip level, give Marlene a thrill when he bent down for things on the bottom shelves.

That day followed in a hideous maze of moaning kids demanding stuff they had seen on telly, shouting stressed out parents, constant demands that he find things, clearing up the mess as kids pulled things off the shelves and dropped them. Janice forever on his back blaming him for stuff getting damaged. It was a total nightmare. Then he found a small girl picking a hole in the plastic cover of a tray of glittery beads and swore at her. She jumped up and started to scream, spilling beads everywhere.

Her parents were there instantly accusing Mervin of everything short of rape, then marched off to see the manager. Mervin was called into the office shortly afterwards and made to apologise to the family. He started to defend himself but was silenced by a furious Mr King. The customer is always right. The family left the store with a free gift and he got a real bollocking and one chance to redeem himself or he was out.

At the end of a momentously lousy day he was getting off the bus back in the town centre when he was joined by Mic and Jaz. Jaz immediately started mincing about and chanting, 'Who's been playing with dollies?' Merv had to hit him, and then swear at an old woman who was watching them, before they slouched down to Fountain Square to hang out with the others.

Just another boring day in the life of a teenage boy.

***

Eric Smith

Eric Smith was born in 1930 and grew up in the county of Berkshire. His early years were spent living in a Victorian cottage where electricity, central heating and television were strangers to him. The cottage boasted a single tap that supplied cold water through lead pipes, while the tin bath hung on a nail outside the back door in the garden.

World War Two dominated his early teens, with the surrounding fields and countryside serving as his playground. It was here that he gained the knowledge and love of nature that plays such a great part in his poems.

Most of his adult life was spent working in a laboratory. Here he gained the art of Microscopy opening the doors to the minute marvels of nature.

He retired to North Devon in 1990 and studied English as a hobby at Bideford Art School. This aroused an interest in creative writing and he wrote his first poems.

Eric says if any of the poems capture the imagination of the reader's mind, then this to him is a satisfactory achievement.

MEETING PLACE

I packed a light lunch, made my way to the bus stop, jumped on and settled down for the journey that would take me to the new meeting place for our friendly creative writing group.

Half an hour later I stepped off at Instow and took my first look at our new writing venue, 'All Saints Chapel'. I was pleasantly surprised to be greeted by a lawned garden tucked discreetly into a tree-surrounded area. There were wooden benches placed so that they overlooked flowering shrubs, while in the centre of the lawn grew a beautiful mulberry tree. This had a circular seat built around the trunk that gave complete shelter from the sun and I was immediately drawn to the welcoming shade and comfort it offered.

As there was nobody about, I took the liberty and sat myself down to eat my lunch. It was so quiet and peaceful and this, with the pleasant surroundings, gave a sense of complete relaxation and contentment. As I sat there I took my first good look at the small neat building standing in one corner offering a unique design. The overall shape was of an oblong but attached to one end was a half round and tapered tower supporting a slate covered roof. This roof was also half round and tapered to a point giving the appearance of a French chateau.

The next thing I observed was the bell tower which was quite high and consisted of a slender square, unfussy column that extended above the roof and divided into a spur. This spur was capped by a slab of stone and from within hung a single bell. The whole building reminded me of many Grecian churches that overlook the olive groves of Greece.

As I studied the building more closely, it began to reveal the more subtle aspects of its design. Running round the top of the walls was a castellated fascia instead of the simple smooth ones that we are used to in this country. The windows were of a stone arched design resting on stone corbels that were in turn supported by columns. The entrance porch was also arched and gave me the impression of half church, half castle. On one corner of the building a ship's lantern was set into a niche. This seemed to me to be out of character yet held a charm of its own.

I was still pondering on the unique design of the building when a woman came to unlock and let us in. As we entered, I was taken aback by the presence of calm and peace the place gave me. The walls were of a plain cream colour broken by a few wrought iron wall lights. The only form of decoration came from an icon wall mural depicting a religious theme. This was painted mainly in blue and captured my eye, drawing me to inspect it. Below was a stone plaque giving the name of a Mr Orphoot who had built the hall in memory of Marjorie Orphoot, his wife, who had died in childbirth.

The crowning beauty of the place lay to the end wall where the recess part of the building had been turned into an altar. I think this area was the most striking part of the building. The altar was of stone and had a fluted front with an ornate frieze. A reredose of grey-green material hung on the wall behind the altar which had a magnificent gold-edged crucifix worked into it. To the sides of the altar, set into the walls, were two plain circular discs with a cross carved into them. Two sedilier type of niches, one under each disc, held vases of flowers (the whole recess of the altar was separated by an altar rail that was capped by a polished mahogany handrail. Above this rail hung a large wrought iron chandelier.)

This was to be our future meeting place and a nicer one I cannot imagine. The rest of the writing group I feel sure are of the same opinion.

IT'S AN ILL WIND

The March wind cut an icy edge through the valley embracing all in its path with a numbing cloak of cold. Intermittent flurries of snow slanted down only to be blown away by the cold wind. A small copse of trees on the far side of the valley threw their gaunt bare arms hard against the skyline's first glimmer of bleak dawn.

Tom Watts stood at the edge of a thicket, his outline masked by the ample thickness of his clothes. A telescopic rifle lay crooked in his right arm, the steel blue of the barrel pointing to the ground. His hands were thrust deep into his pockets to protect them from the cold for he knew that he had to have supple fingers for the job assigned to him. In all his thirty-odd years he had never known a March as cold as this one.

He gazed at the desolate scene in front of him through wind watery eyes and wondered whether the animal would appear. It wouldn't be long now he thought, as the first rays of dawn lit up the drab grey coloured sky.

The local farmer had informed him that the animal always appeared at first light and always from a particular spinney.

The frost-coated fields gave up the last of their moisture as wisps of grey curled from the shallow hollows. Tom pushed his thoughts to the rear of his mind and concentrated on the job he was there to do. Wiping his watery eyes with the back of one hand, he gazed intently into the paling shadows beneath the distant trees. All seemed quiet and still except for the moan of the March wind.

Suddenly there was a slight movement within the darkness of the trees and a huge black creature slowly and nervously emerged. It took a few steps forward and then froze, one forepaw raised in a curled posture as the beast glanced from side to side making sure the coast was clear.

Tom stood admiring the sheer grace and beauty of the animal. The jet black silky fur glistened in the early light enhancing the powerful muscles that rippled beneath the beast's coat. Tom could see the rib cage showing clear while the flanks were hollowed with hunger. The poor beast was half-starved making it bold and fearless. A wave of compassion swept through Tom but he thrust it to one side. He had a job to do and it had to be done.

Slowly and methodically he raised the rifle pressing the butt firmly into his shoulder and swung the barrel onto the beast. He peered through the telescopic sights and focused onto the animal's head. As he did so, the animal turned and seemed to look straight into his eyes. The moment had presented itself. Tom's finger curled round the trigger of the gun, he stopped breathing and relaxed and steadily began to press on the trigger.

Tom took one last look at the animal's face and saw the desperate hunger and misery that showed in the eyes. Slowly he lowered the rifle and let the barrel fall to his side as he realised that he could not bring himself to shoot it.

Tom turned his back on the scene and began to make his way home, glad that he had spared the animal's life. He hoped it would survive as it was not for him to decide whether it should live or die.

He was so engrossed in these thoughts that he never saw or heard as a huge black creature hurled itself from the undergrowth onto his shoulders and bore him down.

*

The valley lay still and quiet except for the long sad moan of the March wind carrying the dismal toll of the village church clock striking the hour.

***

THE DRIFTWOOD'S JOURNEY

You lay splintered, gnarled and twisted
A thing of beauty from the past
Your form the weather has altered
As on sea's burning sands you basked.

Once proud you towered high lordly,
King of all that you surveyed.
Over all you smiled so fondly
At nature's greening accolade.

In a forest of green you flourished
Far from human's grasping hands
Unpolluted air you nourished
Far from ocean's shimmering sands.

Then in raging stormy weather
Wind tore you rough from parent stock
Released from your woody tether
You lay on dark forest floor to rot.

But nature with relentless storms
Bore you in her flooding embrace
From splintered tree so rudely torn
To your new distant resting place.

And so your journey you began
And saw many wondrous sights
To peal of church bells as they rang
Their hymns from belfries stone-built heights.

Eric Smith

Lowing cattle lulled you on your way
Through valleys gentle, quiet, serene.
The scent of new-mown ripening hay
Filled the air with scent fresh so keen.

You hailed strange lands tranquil and green
Fields swaying heavy with golden wheat
Rape glowing yellow you have seen
Soft pastures lined by hedges neat.

Then on the glistening estuary flats
Beneath the brassy blinding sun
Where sand and marram grass enwrap
And twisting tidal channels run.

You lay forlorn, remote, grey, dead,
Half immersed in a watery grave
Your life to lugworms has been wed
Your body washed by sea salt spray.

Your bleached and rotting woody frame,
Now its journey seemed at an end,
Was lashed by angry seas and storms
And lay open to what fate sends.

But man had other plans in mind
And freed you from the estuary's grave.
A thing of beauty to our kind
Your final years in life was saved.

Now in a garden town you lie
With new life you've been endowed.
You bloom bright flowers as you vie
With enhanced beauty, bright and proud.

***

GRANNY'S TEAPOT

My Granny had a teapot
It had a long and drippy spout.
It held lots of boiling water
And was glazed inside and out.

Dark brown was its colour,
Black chipped it was here and there.
But us thirsty, ragged children
Well, we didn't mind or care.

Now my mum worked late on Fridays
So dear Gran kindly took her place.
Her home was clean and tidy
And had a table cloth of lace.

I loved my dear old Granny
And so did my brothers too,
And every Friday we would rush
To her cottage for teatime brew.

Gran welcomed us with gladness,
You could tell she loved us so,
Because her kind old eyes of wrinkled blue
Took on a sparkling warming glow.

Eric Smith

Round the lace topped table we three sat
While Gran brewed the magic tea.
A plate of sticky current buns
Enough for all us hungry three.

Gran would tease us kids continuously
Before pouring tea from the pot,
But once she started it went on
Till we had drunk the blooming lot.

We loved our Friday evenings,
'Twas as good as a day out.
We prayed and eagerly waited
To see again the drippy spout.

Alas those days are over now,
Because tea comes in perforated bags.
Now school's followed by television
Which to me seems very sad.

***

I SHOULD HAVE ASKED

It is too late, the time has passed,
I've been wondering far too long.
Many's the time I should have asked
Before things went awfully wrong.

I didn't know why you were sad,
I never thought to ask, yet care.
I'm sorry that I made you mad
And now my conscience is hard to bear.

When we first had our row and strife
When tears filled your kind loving eye,
I never meant to ruin your life
Or yet to make you sad and cry.

The question that I should have asked
But did not, and I don't know why!
Can you forgive my foolish past?
I plead with you to really try.

That question now I ask of you
What caused the bitter fateful rift?
Tell me my darling and be true
Before I sell the bloody house and shift.

Eric Smith

LETTER FROM AN EXILED FATHER TO HIS SON

As you are there my Son, can you not see
How the cherry blossom hangs, pure white on tree.
Are not your eyes filled with great delight
By the sight of apple blossom's pinkish white?

Does the lark his soaring anthem still sing
With his feathered breast upon the wing.
Have you not heard the cuckoo's two-tone song
As quiet country lanes you strolled along.

Do meadows green still flower in colours bright?
To greet the eye with their glorious sight
While fluffy white clouds fill the wide sky
As April showers cool patter wet by.

Tell me, do the skies still glow wide bright blue
And rainbows arch steep their colourful hues?
Does the village church still toll its single bell?
I remember it all. Oh yes, so well.

Bold hopped the thrush on neat garden lawns,
His liquid song he greeted loud each dawn,
While turtle dove purred soft her sweet call.
How I remember, yes, remember all.

Do the fields of green still grow lush and neat
With daisies dancing white ruffs around one's feet?
How fields of tall, plump golden wheat
Swayed gently beneath the summer's heat.

The rasp of crickets searching for a mate
Used to fill my ears without abate.
The drone of bees that tumbled here and there
Tell me, tell me my son, are they still there?

***

MONDAY BLUES

I stood at the bus stop and gave a slight shiver as the wind and rain buffeted me. I glanced at the leaden grey sky and the dark ragged clouds scudding across its surface. The wind-blown rain hammered against the glass walled surface of the bus stop like peas being shot from a gun.

The empty road glistened in the wetness giving the whole scene a sense of dull drabness devoid of life except for myself. A woman suddenly appeared from the supermarket across the road heavily wrapped in a raincoat. She glanced hurriedly along the street making certain that no traffic was approaching, then crossing over stood by my side in the shelter. After a few moments of awkward silence I ventured to remark about the horrible weather we were having. This was definitely the wrong thing to say as she turned to me and said, 'I expect the bus will be late, it always is when the weather is bad.'

'Never mind,' I replied. 'January will soon be over and then we can look forward to Spring.'

'That's another thing,' she said. 'Spring sets all the birds singing and they wake me up in the morning, so I don't like Spring or the birds.'

I remained silent for a few moments not knowing what to say and then she carried on, 'If it's not the birds then it's my next door neighbour. He's always knocking and banging and waking me up. I don't know why he keeps banging, it annoys me greatly.'

I ventured to pour oil on troubled waters by remarking that she could always turn on the radio and listen to the music.

'I don't like music,' was her reply. 'Especially this modern rubbish, it's all thump, thump, thump. It's worse than the banging and knocking; and as for classical stuff, I don't understand it, it all sounds the same to me.'

At that moment the bus arrived and I stepped on, glad to escape the woman's tirade but to my horror she sat down opposite me. There were a few moments silence and then, 'It's about time they cleaned these windows, you can't see a thing through them.'

I was about to remark that it would be a waste of time cleaning them with the terrible weather we were having when a gentleman came down from the upper deck moaning about it being too cold up top. He took a seat to the rear of the bus and then the woman bent over to me and said, 'I know that man and I don't like him.'

I said, 'Why don't you like him?'

She replied, 'Every time I meet him he is always moaning and groaning.'

***

PICK ME UP

In times of stress when all seems low
And sadness fills the weary soul.
When fortune deals a bitter blow
And deep gloom seems your future goal.

When fate cruelly drags you to your knees
And all seems hopeless with despair.
Then evil thoughts the mind doth tease
To drain the will of hope and care.

Go! seek a good friend's helping hand
For solace, comfort and advice.
Then you will find things will change,
Life will turn from dark to light.

Keep steadfast firm in your beliefs
As living seems to drag you deep in mire.
Let go all tensions, breathe relief.
For better things will soon aspire.

Eric Smith

Swallow your ills, walk tall and true
Refresh your aims and do your best.
Joy through your gloom will soon shine through
To lay your turmoiled mind to rest.

Come! Face the world with all her ills
Embrace each day with new found joy.
Pay up those petty nagging bills
And no more let them annoy.

Be happy in your future ways
Take each day's hurdles as they come.
Be undaunted and be not afraid
And your future joys will be won.

Let not the government get you down
Stand defiant for your human rights.
Enjoy your fortunes, do not frown
Embrace each day with all your might.

***

SCRIPTURE LESSON

I thought I'd read the holy book,
I knew there was a lot to learn.
But my mind was blown right open
And filled with deepest of concern.

The world seemed steeped in hate and greed
Enough to make one lose all hope.
God made the earth for us to love
But we've made it our personal yoke.

In years gone by it was the same
As you can read and surely see.
The world has never really been
As God hopefully meant it to be.

Poor Noah he had nowhere to live
So he built a large wooden boat.
Then filled it full of animals
And then prayed hard that it would float.

Adam and Eve loved their apples
But they were forbidden fruit.
One day they went a-scrumping
But soon rued the price of their loot.

Now Jacob was a local tailor
He made Joseph a coloured coat
From lots of off-cut pieces.
But it wasn't really smart bespoke.

He also scaled a ladder tall
Held up by angels shiny bright.
He fooled his dear old father Isaac
And then fled to the north one night.

Dear old Moses loved his bonfires
He also liked to carve in stone.
He even climbed a mountain steep
Then dragged the heavy slabs back home.

King Pharaoh didn't like the Lord
He simply refused to repent.
So God sent down the heavy mob
Which made the king eager to relent.

David was a lowly shepherd
He could work wonders with a sling.
He slayed the mighty Goliath
And ended up by being king.

Abraham was a psychopath
A very hard nut to crack.
He nearly bumped his own son off
Until God put a stop to that.

Saul was a very jealous man
He hated David's harping skills.
He tried but failed to murder him
But got himself and his son killed.

But let us not give up all hope
Let's blunder blind but bravely on.
Have faith in life and grit your teeth
And do your best to do no wrong.

***

THE CHRISTMAS WONDER

My mum made a Christmas Pudding
Ooh! it were a wondrous thing,
All black, sticky and shiny
And soaked in half a pint of gin.

It had nuts and currants and raisins
Candied peel and a bottle of stout.
It were heavy, rich and shiny
A work of art without a doubt.

Mum knocked it up in a basin
And stirred it with a wooden spoon.
The fumes made us very merry
And peeled the paper off the room.

It took three of us to lift it
It weighed heavy as a piece of lead.
We plonked it in a saucepan
Eight hours of cooking, so mum said.

It heaved and hissed and gave a burp
While we hastily crept away.
We crossed our hearts and said a prayer
And hoped to survive another day.

Eric Smith

It boiled and sulked then heaved about
And swelled up to twice its size.
It glared at us with stodgy hate
Through its black beady currant eyes.

We gazed in fear at the evil mess
As it crept over the edge of the pot.
We then scraped it onto a dinner plate
Oozing jet black and streaming hot.

We poked it with a table fork
To let all the alcohol escape.
It collapsed into a solid lump
And lay quivering with pure hate.

The cat took one sniff then fled in fear
We've never seen the poor thing again.
The dog committed suicide
And the canary went insane.

We used it as a poly-filler
When we decorated the room.
It set hard and solid as a rock
And at night shone like the moon.

***

THE LAWN MOWER

Charlie Banks sat bolt upright on his brand new mower feeling proud as a peacock and raring to go. It was no ordinary mower. Oh no! This one you sat on and rode and didn't have to push. He leaned forward and flicked a spot of dust off the shiny red bonnet with his gor blimey cap then, replacing it on his head, he pondered over who would be the first customer to have the honour of having their lawn cut.

Charlie Banks was a huge barrel of a man with a weather-beaten face that carried a permanent smile. He was slightly flat footed which made him walk with an ambling roll that complimented his appearance. The gor blimey cap he wore seldom left his head and rumour had it that he even wore it in bed. On the rare occasions that he did remove it, a fine shock of silver hair was revealed showing a bald patch in the centre of his head. Charlie was an easy going sort of chap, always laughing and joking and nothing seemed to worry him. Well liked by the village folk and always willing to help if needed.

He only had one job in his life and that was cutting lawns and doing odd jobs around the village. With his easy going disposition he never seemed to lose his temper or yet to worry.

Now Charlie had never driven a ride-on mower before. He had always been content with an ordinary walk and push type, but as he reached old age he had found it hard going and so had splashed out on a sit on and drive type.

He decided to cut the church cemetery grass first. This would give him plenty of practice as he weaved in and out between the tombstones. Starting up the engine he eased the mower through the church lychgate and onto the grass. He adjusted the cutting height and pressed down on the accelerator. Without warning the mower leapt forward like a bat out of hell and churned through two headstones. Charlie rammed on the brakes, climbed off the mower, raised his gor blimey cap, scratched his head and replaced it back on. He heaved the flattened headstones back into position and stamped firmly on the ruts the mower wheels had made. The thought went through his mind; people usually get run over first and then get buried not the other way around. Never mind, he thought, I'll come back later and put things right, nobody will notice. Climbing back onto the mower he finished mowing the grass and only broke a couple of vases and churned up two wreaths.

Mrs Jones lived next door to the church so Charlie decided to cut her lawn next. Opening her garden gate he started to inch his way into the garden. There was an almighty crash as the back of the mower snagged the gate post and pulled gate and post out of alignment. Off came the cap, head scratched, back went the cap. 'Oh well! never mind I will fix it when I do the tombstone,' he thought. He carried on and cut the woman's lawn and had only one more mishap as he managed to reduce the rhubarb to lawn level.

The next job was the vicarage. He was determined to make a good job of this as the vicar had often recommended him to people. He was beginning to feel his way with the mower by now and he soon finished the job. It was a shame about the daffodils though, but after all they would flower again next year and who would have thought that a man of the cloth would have used such language like that. Never mind he mused, cap raised, head scratched, cap replaced.

Charlie decided to do one more job and then call it a day. After all one mustn't become over confident as that's how accidents occur.

Sir Hugh Asquith was his next customer and as Charlie sat on his mower he eyed the large lawn in front of him. Nothing could go wrong here, why there were no flower borders or shrubs to worry about, just a long and wide lawn surrounded by the garden fence. Full of confidence he rammed his foot down and flew down the lawn at full speed. Charlie was filled with exhilaration, air rushed past his face, and the ground seemed to tear past his feet. Eyes gleaming in excitement he rocketed down the lawn until he reached the fence. He rammed his foot down on the brake, his foot slipped and Charlie and mower went straight through the fence to the sound of shattering timber and finally came to rest with the mower in the middle of the greenhouse. Cap off, head scratched, cap back on.

Charlie understood why Sir Hugh was upset but how was he to know that the mangled remains beneath the mower were prize carnations ready for the flower show tomorrow.

***

THE STONE WALL

The hard grey surface of the pavement reflected the sun's heat penetrating the soles of Jack Spicer's shoes playing havoc with his corns. An empty buckled Coca Cola tin rattled its erratic way along the gutter, its metallic tune matching its ugliness. Globs of squashed chewing gum littered the pavement in large white blobs mimicking the pigeons' guano. Rain stained cigarette butts thrown down by uncaring people complimented the chewing gum.

Gusts of warm dust laden air blew through the vandalised bus stop that was minus a pane of glass. The bench seat was bent and sagging, making it uncomfortable to sit on. A Morrisons plastic shopping bag was wrapped around a lamp post where the wind had blown it.

A car sped down the high street pumping bucketfuls of rock and roll music from its open window. The driver gave a loud blast on the horn as he spotted one of his mates on the pavement. His mate responded with a loud cheer and a wave as the car revved and roared away out of sight. The wail of an ambulance cut through the noisy cries of the gulls as the driver raced home to dinner. Two large pennants affixed to lamp posts read,

WELCOME TO BIDEFORD

It was at this moment that Jack spotted the blue door, it was set into a long stone wall and was the only thing that broke the ugly monotonous surface. Curiosity led Jack to examine it closer. The door was constructed entirely of metal with a small gridded window set into it that was too high for him to peer through. The door was probably painted blue to help break up the featureless monotony of the drab wall.

The Stone Wall

As Jack stood looking at it, Oscar Wilde's Poem, 'The Ballad Of Reading Gaol,' sprang to mind. The stanza that reads:

> 'I never saw a man who looked with such a wistful eye,
> upon that little tent of blue that prisoners call the sky.'

An overwhelming urge made Jack stretch forth his hand and try the handle. To his surprise it yielded to his touch. He knew he was about to trespass but couldn't resist the temptation to open the door and enter. Before him stretched a long undulating lawn that sparkled with the morning's glistening dew. The air seemed to vibrate with life yet gave a sense of peace and serenity. Everything seemed to glow with an ethereal calmness. Trees whispered their joy to breezes high as they sang their quiet song of contentment.

Before he realised what he was doing he had removed his socks and shoes to let the damp dew bathe his feet in its coolness. From the flower borders, blooms greeted him in a galaxy of colour. The scent of hyacinths, mixed with the smell of new mown grass, pervaded his nostrils, charming him with its heavy sweetness.

A blackbird hopped and ran on the lawn, his yellow bill and circled eye contrasting with his black body. A chaffinch hurled his tumbling hard to morning's smile while a robin poured his poignant melody from a flaming shield of red.

Jack was lost in this wonderland of nature's splendour. He knew not where he wandered nor yet cared. Butterflies waved banners bright to the tune of insects' drowsy drone. A nearby waterfall laughed its chuckling clear, its crystal flow cascading over moss grown boulders to waters clear at its feet. Jack stood spellbound and humble at all he saw and knew that creation had laid her hand on all.

It was at that moment that he saw a man approaching him and Jack thinking that it was the owner began to apologise for trespassing. The man held up his arm and said, 'There is no need to apologise, and if you wish I will show you the way to the blue door.'

As they approached the door Jack remarked, 'It is a pity to leave such beauty behind.' The man placed his hand on Jack's shoulder and said, 'There is no need to leave, everyone who enters that door is given the choice to leave or to stay. It is up to each person to make their own decision.'

An ambulance wailed its way to a stop alongside the stone wall. Lying on the pavement was the body of a man curled up in front of a blue door. Two Paramedics climbed out of the ambulance, opened the rear doors and carrying a stretcher over to the collapsed man proceeded to place him on the stretcher. The paramedics thought the man must have been overcome by the heat and must have collapsed on the pavement. What they couldn't understand was why the man was barefooted and where had his socks and shoes gone.

As the ambulance sped on its way to the hospital an old buckled Coca Cola tin was caught in the ambulance back draught and rolled on its rattling way.

***

TORCH

I was one among the many people noisily thronging the street that day. The day the 'Olympic Torch' was to be borne through the town.

Standing at the edge of the pavement I glanced at the happy people lining the road. Joy and excitement pervaded everywhere with waving flags and banners all in anticipation of the great occasion. Suddenly a cheer arose along the street. Necks craned to view the arrival but it turned out to be farmer Brown driving his very smelly muck spreader on the way to his farm. He soon passed but the smell lingered on.

There was a slight commotion and peering round I was faced by a small girl seated in a wheelchair trying to find a space where she could see the arrival. We hurriedly made room for her (it was not for us to deny her the once in a lifetime event) and were rewarded by a grateful smile from her small pale face.

Patiently we waited while the idle chatter amongst us helped to pass the time. Suddenly there was a loud cheer from the crowds along the road and we knew that at last the big moment had arrived. The cheering grew nearer and nearer, the volume louder and louder. A wave of expectation seemed to ripple through the crowd. Bodies tensed and straining. Excitement high. Flags and banners were waving frantically and all seemed delirious in anticipation.

Then he appeared, dressed all in white, golden cone held high above his head like a messenger bearing all the cherished hopes of the people. Slowly he advanced, drawing closer and closer until he came opposite to the little girl in the wheelchair. He spotted her and, without a moment's hesitation, walked over to her. Bending down on one knee (so as to bring himself to her height) he held the torch out and in a quiet voice said, 'There you are my dear, hold it tight in both hands.' Her small, frail arms reached out eagerly, hands curled in readiness, eyes fixed on the cone. Ten tiny fingers curled themselves around it. Her small dark eyes dilated in wonderment and joy and my whole world stood still.

As the bearer arose so then did my emotions as I watched with misted eyes as bearer and torch were carried along the road with all the dreams and hopes of one small girl and the people along with it.

Turning my back, I slowly made my way home realising that two acts had been played out that day. One being that there was still hope for the future, the other was that there still remained compassion for our fellow beings. There was no doubt whatsoever in my mind. Truly this had made my day.

***

WHY

They touched my hand, they queried why
And what it was that made me cry.
I was in a church deep in thought
Subdued in peace the quiet had brought.

When softly drifting loud and clear
Came treble notes of chorister near
In voice that stole the higher notes
Trembled rapture from a single throat.

Such poignant singing pierced my being
That tears welled up to blur my seeing.
I touched their hands and they knew why
'*Allegris Miserere*' made me cry.

They held my hand, they asked me why
And how it was some others cried?
Fresh summer mornings, bright and clear
With sight of otter, hare or deer.

Streams flowing over boulders leap
In fields with gentle grazing sheep,
Here misty vale and valleys deep
God's wildlife his dominions keep.

And as they marvel at what they spy
So watery veils blot out their eye,
I held their hands, they realised why
Nature's beauty made others cry.

They pressed my hand and told me why
And what it was that made all cry
If laid low in despair or pain
No words of comfort, hope or gain.

Eric Smith

When misery denies us sleep
With only ourselves our grief to keep.
When tears well up from body deep
In tune to heaving shoulders keep.

I'll press their hands and tell them why
They should grasp our outstretched hands
And help so that
we need not cry.

They embraced my hands, and I knew why
Pure love and beauty made all cry.
Two loving hearts both full of grace
Seeing only beauty in each other's face.

Two minds entwined as though in one
To evil thoughts will not succumb.
But should this bond ever die
Then surely it would make us cry?

As for beauty in nature's realm
It lies before us all around.
It is our duty to preserve
This gift, this earth, this universe.

Lose love, lose beauty, let these die?
Surely that would make all humans cry
I embraced their hands, they said goodbye,
I felt the tears flow from my eye.

***

THE VILLAGE CHURCHYARD

In sleepy hollow set in fields of green
Where time hangs slow from world's rush and care
Quiet lies a churchyard, old, beside a stream
Where nature blooms her green and pleasant ware.

Along cool grassy banks the stream flows slow
Celandines dance bright their yellow delight
Cool gentle breeze through spiky rushes grow
And dragonflies dance swift their colours bright.

Between the old yew trees lie shadows deep
Here ivy trails her creeping tendrils long
While wild roses coy their blush pink do peep
And daisies smile white ruffs in thick gay throngs.

Oak trees pin dark their aged and twisted arms
Hard to the deep blue open sweeping sky
Proud stands the church with all its ancient charms
Where souls in peaceful rest forever lie.

Jackdaws chack sharp their scold of discontent
When church bell tolls loud its bronze lament
Belfry thrusts grey toward the heavens' elements
While headstones lean heavy their grave intent.

Beneath each couch of soil around my feet
Sleeps a part of England's majestic past
Here once a yeoman's faithful heart did beat
True to England's mighty reign, held fast.

Dear God; may this isle remain forever free
And let's defend our hard-won human rights
To live in peace, goodwill and harmony
In a future of love and delight.

***

Richard J Small

An overrated writer, hardly worth looking at his work unless you are an insomniac and short of tranquilisers. Opinionated, inordinately dry sense of humour, attempts drama and adventure but you'll find it more exciting opening a bag of crisps and possibly more interesting. Not recommended for ordinary people or those with a mind of their own.

A MOUNTAIN TO CLIMB

Compelled by worsening weather, he rested a while on his climb. He reached out with a trembling hand to a wall of stone to check his balance, his ankles twisting as they adjusted to the slope. Quietly, almost impossibly, he gasped for breath. It was as though the air he breathed had thinned, his muscles ached and his joints pained him like never before. But he must climb on, he cannot stop here, he must continue. Easing the pressure on his old shoulders from the thin straps of a worn canvas rucksack he began once more up the slope, the deep snow under his thin leather boots, now crisp with frost. A bitingly cold wind blew over the ridge from the east. It would have almost been a blessing if his hands were numb with cold but all he felt was a relentlessly fierce pain through his woefully inadequate woollen gloves. The unseasonably bad weather had taken him somewhat by surprise, as too had his own age and ability to make a climb so easily done in his youth. He'd been a good climber once, a keen sportsman, always striving to succeed and lift the trophy, even if only for a photo at the finish. Now, was a struggle of epic proportions, the trophy at the end of this climb was life itself, to fail was death. He was alone - this was not the place for thrill seekers, for even they were safe at home. Every agonising step was an enormous struggle, each one was short and laboured, the wind tugged at his clothes trying to confound him but he was solemnly resolute, it was only he that could save himself.

He stopped again, gathered his remaining strength and then plodded on inexorably, miserably, even tearfully, his stooped body leaning into the hill before him. This was no glorious race, with the eyes of the world watching with bated breath, this was a lonely private struggle for which he only had himself to blame, the only eyes that watched were those of Angels, wringing their helpless hands in pity and sorrow.

He was no stranger to this place, he was just a stranger to the circumstances, in a self reflective moment he remembered how strong he was in his youth. Recalling those youthful days had helped him a little, bolstered his spirits and squinting past his frosted eyelashes he could just make out the summit. It wasn't so far now. Not in distance perhaps but in time it seemed like a million miles. Darkness would soon be on him and drag him down like a pack of black Hyenas, if he falls he may not be able to rise again, he must not fail - it is not yet his time. His tired muscles, weak with age and cramped with burned out effort hardly responded to his desperate call.

Finally, only moments to spare with the fast closing shadow of the grim reaper behind him on the slope, he arrived. He kicked off the snow from his boots, shut the door behind him and shuffled through to a warm kitchen and the kettle. He placed his rucksack on the table and picked something out for tea.

Pensioner and widower, 87 year old Edmund Scott, was home from the shops.

Story inspired by watching an elderly gentleman in the street expending all his effort merely to make his way home. You too must have seen these warriors of age in their daily battles. Give them a thought. April 2016 Devon

***

THE LOVE OF LIFE - LOUISA

(Inspired by the lifeboat, Louisa of Lynmouth, in the late 19th century, when lifeboats were launched by man and horse and were rowed to the scene.)

Wild calls for help, bring with them fear; maroons, they wake the night. Calls, to men both brave and strong and bound by hope, not fright. The crew is picked, the orders clear, the coxswain shares his plan. She's launched into the pounding surf, as only life boats can.

'Pull hard my crew,' the coxswain shouts, 'Pull hard for distant sail. Through wind and wave and darkness, I vow that we'll not fail.' Back at the quay, the helpers stand. When will the storm abate? To welcome heroes home again, their fearful hearts must wait.

Upon the ship the children cry, the tattered sails cry too. Their captain tired, he's given up, not so, the lifeboat crew. 'Set off a flare,' the coxswain says; 'Twas done without a fuss. As dark turned bright, the captain prayed, 'God's angels come for us.'

Then voices called from out the dark, 'You're saved, now come aboard,' but robbed of prize and sacrifice, the angry sea, it roared. The ropes were thrown, and grapnel fast, ship's timber it did grip. With failing hands and racing hearts they stumbled from their ship.

As one by one they made their way, each felt the need to rush. The sea, it wants to hurry too, Louisa's hull to crush. They sigh relief and comfort seek, all huddled on the deck. Now spirits high and bent to oars they leave the sinking wreck.

Photo from a painting
by Mark Meyers RMSA

Now turned for shore and distant lights, oh, still so far from home and homeward bound, they have to race, white horses, and the foam. The waves rise high and troughs sink deep, the elements do rave, determined not to let them go, but put them in their grave.

That coxswain strong had other thoughts; he'd seen it all before. 'Our good Louisa life boat, will take us to the shore.' While sound of surf at base of cliff, bids the storm run free, to know if they can make it home, they pray; as so might we.'

***

THE CHRISTMAS CARD

Five days I watched the letter box,
and not a thing came though.
Then seventeen came all at once,
though sadly, none from you.

Such fears as come with policeman's knock,
not knowing, why or how,
and still I long to hear your news,
so missed in life, right now.

Bright envelopes of every size,
to open each, a thrill.
With eighty seven on display,
there's one, I wait for still.

***

THE RESOLUTE COXSWAIN
(A lifeboat rescue story like no other.)

Old George Millar was a popular grocer in the little fishing village of Dugenen. His shop, with its worn boarded-floor and evocative smells of package-free food and spices, was like a place that time had left behind. Now in his eightieth year, kindly George Millar still served, driven on by a secret he'd kept for fifty years, compelled by conscience never to give up.

George straightened the worn collar of his soft and comfortable shop coat, returned to the wooden counter and added freshly cut cheese to the contents of his customer's cotton shopping bag. 'There you go, young Andrew, you'll not be short of something for tea now and just the job for a snack after a call out. Has the boat been busy lately?'

Andrew, with several years experience at sea, was second coxswain for the village's all-weather lifeboat. It was a job he loved dearly and like many of his forebears always felt he was born to it. 'No, nothing much happened this week, Mr Millar, just a shout to surfers who were taken along the shore by the rip tide. Just as well that it's quiet too, this being early March, the skipper is away for a week's training in Dorset, possibly a new boat coming our way later in the year is my guess. Mind you, the weather forecast is not good for later today. Rapidly strengthening winds with a cold front from the east they say, that'll keep the surfers on shore, even the wild ones.'

'And indoors in some nice warm hostelry no doubt,' smiled the affable old shopkeeper, 'and who could blame them?' Then his face darkened and the smile disappeared, 'Of course, I knew your grandfather Robert well. A dreadfully sad day it was when we lost him. He was a first-rate coxswain and a good man indeed. When the alarm beckoned him to sea for some poor soul in need, you never found him wanting, he wouldn't give up until he found them you know. Might be what cost him so dear in the end.' George was staring intently at an empty space in the shop as though looking in disbelief at a wild but empty ocean, to this day still looking frantically for some sign of a life that was already long extinguished. 'It was a day much like this one Andrew, I tell you, just like this one.' George Millar often repeated his sad tale, forgetting he'd told it so many times before. From that day on, he'd lived racked with a sense of guilt and a haunting memory from which this old man could not be free.

Andrew always humoured him, never letting on. They all knew how George Millar had punished himself all these years, 'I don't remember him, Mr Millar, I'm sad to say he died before I was old enough. Dad has told me many a tale of his exploits though, so I feel that I do know him. We have a few photographs of course and I almost see him before me when dad tells his stories. I suppose his tales are born of truth, duty and tragedy and as such, they always carry something of the spirit with them, something undying. They're stories that will live forever. Both stood humbly quiet for a minute or more, their shared silence suddenly broken by a rapid bleeping. Instinctively Andrew slipped the pager from his belt and read the message. . . it simply said, 'launch all-weather boat.'

'Must go Mr Millar, we've got a shout, keep my groceries for me, see you later,' and with that the old shop door rattled closed and he was gone.

'Stay safe boy, stay safe,' muttered George. He knew only too well what might be waiting for his brave friends in the gathering storm. A gust of wind beat at his shop door. George Millar sighed. Picking up the bag to place it in the fridge, he muttered to himself, 'A day just like this, just like this.'

Andrew was not first to arrive at the lifeboat station, the mechanic was already there and dressed. Engine running, the tractor was parked on the slipway with the transfer boat waiting on its trailer.

'Local boat called it in, Andrew. It's the *Anne-Clare*, crew of three, one man overboard, half mile off the west point of Anchor Rocks, they have fishing gear out and retrieving it now,' he shouted, pointing to a sheet of paper he held out towards Andrew.

Andrew lifted a hand in silent acknowledgement and entered the locker room to collect his waterproofs and life jacket. 'Fishing gear out,' he thought. 'That'll slow them up, no wonder they've called for us.'

Andrew knew Mark, the skipper of the *Anne-Clare*, quite well, they'd been to school together. Some of Mark's family had also served on the village's earlier lifeboats, *Princess Dauntless* and the *Jocelyn*. It was a sad *Princess Dauntless* that had slunk home from the sea without his grandfather all those years before.

Andrew shook himself out of such thoughts and called for a crew of six from the rapidly gathering volunteers. Integrity and a common purpose overriding any personal desires or fears, it was not long before the chosen few were afloat and motoring out in the transfer boat to the deep water channel. There, like a straining dog on a leash, the Tamar-class lifeboat rocked impatiently in the waves as though eager to be slipped from her mooring.

They faced a spring tide, running strong and rising fast at nearly half flood. Conditions that meant the ocean currents around Anchor Rocks would be even more dangerous than usual. They were going to have to hurry, the weather would undoubtedly worsen.

By the time the crew were pulling themselves aboard, the bustling cloud had already thickened overhead and a cold wind sprang up from the east, a woeful harbinger of rain. As the crew hurried efficiently about their tasks, the boat's great diesel engines roared into life like a rudely awakened giant. As it was untied and readied to return to the slipway and safety, the impatient transfer boat bumped roughly against the lifeboat's deep blue hull. Even in the estuary there was a rapidly rising swell.

'Shore boat's away, Cox,' called the deck crew as the navigator took his place and prepared his sea charts for the journey.

'Standby to let go mooring,' Andrew eased the throttles forward, for slack on the mooring shackle.

'Free for'ard,' came the snappy reply above the strengthening wind. As the boat cleared the buoy and started out along the estuary, the mechanic busied himself with the radio. 'Coastguard, coastguard, coastguard, this is lifeboat *Dauntless II*, crew of six, now at sea and mobile to man over board, fishing vessel *Anne-Clare*, Anchor Rocks, over.'

It was a good five mile run to the incident, a tough five miles that first took them out into the bay and then North to the rocky promontory called Anchor Point. An Atlantic ground swell added to wave heights, peaking around ten feet or more, limiting their speed to about fifteen knots. Maybe a twenty or thirty minute journey and every one of them a living hell for their friend lost at sea.

'*Anne-Clare, Anne-Clare, Anne-Clare*, this is the lifeboat, *Dauntless II*, at sea and on course for your last position, are you receiving, over?'

Meanwhile, the lifeboat left the relative calm of the estuary and began to hit the open sea beyond the sand bar. Andrew steered a course with port bow to the waves, it might lessen the crew's discomfort. Visibility was reduced by spray that topped the waves like flowing manes of the sea's wild white horses, wind beating against tide created over-falls and spindrift on the crests of deep green waves; a translucent deep green, a beautiful captivating colour that enticed, and commanded attention. Then came the eagerly awaited reply. '*Dauntless II, Dauntless II, Dauntless II*, this is the fishing vessel *Anne-Clare*, good to hear your voice. We have our fishing gear all aboard now, visibility poor and worsening. Bob Harkness went overboard about forty minutes ago. The only good news is that he was wearing foul-weather gear and life-jacket at the time. With only two of us left on board we are unable to search for him with any degree of safety.'

Most of the lifeboat crew knew Bob Harkness; a likeable young man with a family and many friends in the local community. Andrew spoke resolutely and quietly to his mechanic and navigator, 'Find his exact position now, then see what the current might have done with young Bob since their first call. Let Mark know, we won't let him down, soon be there, then his keen eyes were back on the green and white of a wild and growing sea that stretched away into an uncertain future.

Meanwhile, old George Millar looked pensively out of his shop window at the changing sky, 'Just like today,' he mumbled, his thoughts far away. Head down and shuffling his weary feet slowly across the seemingly rolling floor boards, it might as well have been yesterday, it was all so clear to him. He leant forward to press his hands on the counter edge just as forty years before he'd pressed them on the storm soaked rail of the *Princess Dauntless*. 'Some fool in a cabin cruiser – no right to be out there! Idiot!' He paused from his brief anger and was aware of being back in his shop, the wind rattling the door as if to wake him from his recurring nightmare. But he was soon at sea again, raging green waves with spindrift conspired to rob lost souls of any rescue. Eventually they'd come across the hapless small boat by sheer luck. She was starting to founder, rolling more and more, deeper and deeper. To all the crew, brave indeed as they were, it looked a certain lost cause. But Robert, their coxswain would have none of it, resolute he was, he would never give up, never. Neither could he bring himself to ask anyone to do what he wouldn't do himself. 'George,' he'd said, 'here, take the helm.' With George now at the controls, Robert made his way to the rail and, with an almost beyond human effort, boarded the stricken vessel. For a moment the crew saw his intense eyes searching, earnestly searching for a sign of life. Then suddenly that silly damned boat rolled hard on a wave and capsized. Not long after that she slid deep from sight.

George was overwhelmed by the haunting memories he'd carried alone for too many years, aware that he must finally tell what he knew, someone must hear his tale. 'Oh, we searched and we searched for our beloved coxswain until fuel and us was near exhausted. I swear on my life I saw him once, in a deep, fleeting trough, still wearing sou'wester and high enough in the water to see his life vest. Oh, I shouted and pointed but it was only I could see him. He was waving us away - gesturing for us to leave him in that watery hell and go home. I'll never know the truth of it. His image haunts me to this day, a day just like this. Some there were that praised him for his bravery and some there were that cursed him for the very same, leaving us like he did. His body was never found and to this day the sea still has him. Our dear Robert is still out there somewhere.'

Putting on his coat and hat, George Millar left the shop, locked the door and slowly made his way to a place he once knew so well, the lifeboat station by the old quayside. He tucked in his scarf, turned up his collar and wiped a tear from his eye with a worn sleeve. How could he ever forget?

'There she is, off the port bow,' came the lookout's cry, as the *Anne-Clare* came into sight. Andrew was decisive, 'Radio to Mark to hold his course and speed steady, we're coming close alongside, make ready the crew to move up to the flying bridge.' At the same time, he dropped a few revolutions off the powerful engines and deftly brought *Dauntless II* around to run parallel and on the windward side of the rolling fishing vessel. They were close enough to shout across and gather useful information, enough to initiate a search pattern that gave them at least some prospect of locating the lost fisherman.

High up from the lifeboat's flying bridge, all eyes scanned the chaos of a boiling sea. All were eager and ready to shout and point the moment they found young Bob.

Motoring on, above an insatiable ocean, the valiant crew's rescue boat pitched and rolled steeply on a giant cloak of deep green as though Neptune was shaking it himself. At fifteen minutes gone, the navigator voiced his grave concerns, 'Look, Andrew, we've near enough completed the official designated search pattern and we're edging closer all the while to the sunken rocks off the Point. As we have wind over tide I think the current may have taken him closer to shore but the wind will have moved the *Anne-Clare* relatively further out to sea. We won't have much time.'

With time and tide in a deadly race against them, Andrew decided on a couple of sweeps closer inshore and nearer the treacherous submerged rocks off the Point, then failing that they would be obliged to repeat the already unsuccessful standard search pattern.

It was not going well at all. Visibility was already appalling. Nothing found inshore, they began to motor seawards again, when suddenly Andrew caught a glimpse of someone in the water, he began to shout, 'We have him!' but went deathly quiet when he realised this was not their friend Bob. No, this man was older, wearing clothing from a bye-gone age . . . and under an old sou'wester, his face shared a knowing smile. The old man in the water was pointing insistently and resolutely towards the next wave. Then he was gone. Andrew said nothing about his vision to the crew. Regardless of cold logic that would have ignored the apparition, his soul made him look where he'd been told. Sure enough, as they crested the next wave, there in the trough was the lost fisherman. The shout went up in preparation to gather him safely on board.

Poor Bob Harkness had been in the water for what seemed to him an eternity. Spray stinging his face, fingers numbed to useless, cold biting deep into the bones of his body - he did not expect to survive. He knew any chance of being found in such a chaotic sea was against all the odds, it was a risk they all accepted when they took such work. Pulling his knees up to conserve what little heat he had left, alone and afraid he waited for the end to come. His heart had already sunk beneath the waves nearly an hour before, when he'd tumbled overboard, watching helplessly as the *Anne-Clare* motored away into the waves without him. Now, finally he'd succumbed to a strange quietness - just waiting for the deep to swallow him up.

Bob was completely unaware of the lifeboat's presence and its gentle, beam on approach from behind him. That is until he thought he heard, 'Come on dopey, we haven't got all day you know.' To begin with he ignored the voice, for earlier he

The Resolute Coxswain

thought he'd already seen and heard things in the nearby sea. Somewhat unnerving it was. As his body sank into a wave trough something told him he was not alone. Like an old friend's voice calling to him on the wind. Then the voice came again, only louder, 'Oi! Don't you want a lift home then Bob? You'll go all wrinkly if you stay out here much longer!'

A shivering Bob flailed his cold, tired arms and legs weakly to turn around. Thank you God; he was saved; smiling friendly faces, arms reaching out, and the rescue sling already in the water for him. Tonight he would dine with his wife and children and not with Davy Jones. Soon, secure on board and being treated for the exposure, he smiled thankfully as he could feel the powerful diesel engines carrying them like a caring father would his small child, safely away from danger.

Still on emergency channel 16, the mechanic radioed their success to the coastguard and conveyed a message to the fishing vessel.

Dauntless II, now making way with the tide, managed an easy seventeen knots. They were going home; every single one of them.

Even as they moored *Dauntless II* to the deep channel buoy, the shore boat was alongside. Bob Harkness would be taken away first to a waiting ambulance and despite his emotional protestations, attend the County Hospital for the mandatory check up.

After closing down, checking fuel and securing the lifeboat, Andrew and his brave volunteers were also ferried ashore. As he walked into the station, the first man Andrew met was old George Millar, 'Hi Mr Millar, what brings you down here? You brought my groceries?'

'I had to come. It was a day just like this when we lost your grandfather. I never told you did I, never told anyone,' he said, gesturing Andrew away to one side for privacy, 'but I thought I saw him in the water that day you know, waving us away, I can still see him now, like as though he'll pop into my shop any day. . . He was never one to give up, and yet we came home safe without him, we left him behind, we lost him to the deep.'

'Never you mind Mr Millar, you're a special man yourself, we all think we see things in the sea, in fact I believe I saw him myself today. He showed me where to find our Bob Harkness when all seemed lost for certain. Funny, he looked just like my dad described, had a smile on his face too he did. He never did give up did he? Perhaps his spirit is still out there looking for souls to save.' Andrew touched the old man's shoulder with a strong hand, 'Best we tell no one else though, eh Mr Millar, best we keep it to ourselves, or else they'll be locking us both up! I'll get out of this wet gear and walk back with you to the shop, collect my tea things.'

At last our old friend George finally understood the truth of the apparition he saw that fateful day so long ago. One lost soul was grief enough for the village to bare but an entire crew lost on a fool's errand would be a pointless tragedy. Robert's resolute and abiding spirit had urged him to take the crew safe home to live and serve again. At long last George Millar's own soul could be at peace once more.

He smiled and knew, 'There'll never be another day like this, not like this one.'

***

THE TRAVELLER'S CONFESSION

Aged 84 he'd run his course and he knew it, his bones were old and weak. A kindly fire warmed his life-tired body and what he knew would be his last supper. He'd learned the hard way how to leave the dearly loved behind him and never return, never to tell. He'd been no stranger to loneliness most of his life, though it didn't start that way.

His old horse was now tether-free in the field and would doubtless find a good home such was his nature, as would his old dog, noble companion for some six years now.

As he gazed though the light smoke at his faithful old dog, he wished such loyalty had been part of his earlier life. However, now was the time to tell what had remained a secret these forty years. 'Well, my dear old pal,' John said quietly, as if others might overhear, his dog obliged by cocking an ear and tilting his head to one side, 'My early years were bathed in riches and privilege. We had a grand house in Belgravia and vast estates in Mayo. Life was good, I knew no other. I married, we had a lovely son and we had servants to look after us. It was one of them that changed my life. She had come by some gossip of which I'd known nothing, nor could I entertain. She threatened to disclose an affair between my mother and a traveller who frequented our lands in Mayo. True or not, to protect my mother and the man I knew as father, as well as my wife and son, she had to be silenced. In silencing her, I was overwhelmed by consequences that hadn't occurred to me. I had to run, so run I did. I made my way to the country estate in Mayo which I knew so well from childhood days. I found the old traveller that I'd often seen watching me in those early, care free childhood years. I spoke with him; it was easy unburdening my worries on a stranger with no connections to courts, police or what we foolishly call civilised society. He understood, he was kindly and he took me in, he showed me the ways of the traveller. In truth he was as good as any father could be to a son. Before he breathed his last he asked me to break with tradition and not burn his caravan. For I was to use it and safely live out a worthy life as best I could, knowing travelling was in my blood.'

The fire was dying; he no longer felt like eating supper. He would light a candle and rest in his bed and dream of better days. He stood shakily and patted his old dog gently on the head, 'Some things are sadly missed in life old boy, sadly missed indeed.'

As the mists of morning rose, the old dog lay quietly by the warm embers of a once proud traveller's caravan and in the ashes, Lord Lucan kept his secret still.

FATE AND THE NIGHT OF THE CARDS

Rowena, cup and plate in hand, walked from her modest living room to wash her tea time dishes in the kitchen. A gentle, almost reticent knocking at her front door stopped her dead in her tracks.

She walked inquisitively along the boarded hallway to the front door of her humble terraced house. The door opened directly onto the pavement outside, where the evening mist conspired with the dim street lights to colour the deserted road a shadowy urban grey.

She tidied her shawl around her shoulders, then opened the door cautiously. Before it was fully open, a man's voice inquired, 'Mrs Henderson? Mrs Rowena Henderson?'

There seemed no menace in the man's voice and she answered, 'Yes, that's me. What can I do for you?'

'I saw your compelling advert in the post office window, the one advertising card readings, I'm afraid I talked the shop keeper into telling me where you lived, sorry. I know it is an imposition... you can say no, if you like, but please don't... I really need a card reading; it must be tonight, there may never be another chance.'

His voice sounded more desperate and hopeful than dangerous to Rowena, so she stood to one side of the doorway and said, 'Well dear, you'd better come through then, it's getting damp out there and we can't read cards on the doorstep can we?' Rowena closed the door securely and ushered him along the short hallway to the one presentable room she used for general living.

'Pop your coat on the back of that chair and sit yourself at the table,' said Rowena clearing a space and reaching for a pack of cards from a drawer. 'What shall I call you? And what exactly is it you want to find out?' she asked with a smile.

The questions noticeably surprised him, as if he wasn't expecting any questions coming his way. . . 'er, call me John. . . and what ever you tell me will be what I want. I'll leave it all in your hands. Thank you.'

'Okay John, just hold this pack of cards for me, use both hands, we don't want to miss anything do we? I'll be back in a moment. I'll just put the kettle on.'

Public card reading was a new and enforced venture for her. She was short of money since she and her husband had parted company. He was an addicted gambler, not a bad man other than that, but the gambling was all to live and die for and the distress had been too much for her to endure, so she'd rented this little house and begun a new life. Rowena worked in a local care home and, as she had been adept from childhood at reading cards, thought she might supplement her income with a few readings. She asked John if he would like a cup of tea. He nodded in reply but once again appeared nervous and was taking an intrusive interest in the contents of the room, particularly Rowena's family photos.

Rowena was becoming uneasy, 'Steady on old girl,' she calmed herself silently, 'stay composed and don't let on, everything will be fine, come on, take the tea in, light a candle and put the bright light out, then he can't be nosing around the room with his prying eyes. I wonder who he really is, perhaps the cards will tell.'

The cups chinked in the saucers and the bright light was replaced by a warming candle flame. 'Do you live alone then, Mrs Henderson?' asked John, as though he already knew the answer.

'Yes, and I have done for nearly a year now,' Rowena replied, at once regretting not saying that she didn't and her burly ex-army husband would be arriving home at any minute. But it wasn't her way, she was inherently kind and honest. 'Come on now John, if you want this card reading you must concentrate; relax but concentrate on the matter in hand. I want you to shuffle the pack, any way you like, just shuffle the cards and think on your questions.'

**

'Right John, keeping the cards face down I'd like you now to pick ten cards from the pack, it doesn't matter how you do it; if you wish you can spread them all over the table. It will almost feel like the card chooses you. You will just know the right ones. Take your time.'

Rowena watched as the stranger's strong, rough hands hovered over various cards then struggled to pick them up with his short fingernails, but she didn't intervene and he seemed to have considerable patience. Eventually John picked ten cards and held them up triumphantly, 'there, they all picked me, just like you said they would Mrs Henderson. Amazing, I've never had a card reading before, I just knew which ones to avoid and which to pick. I can already see this is going to be well worth my while.'

'Okay John, now I want you to make sure that the cards are in the right order, you need to use the same feeling you had when you picked them, shuffle or move them about until something tells you the order feels right to you,' Rowena said quietly as she finished her now lukewarm tea. She leant back in her chair, observed his mannerisms and his obvious lack of card handling skills, it made her wonder why a card reading was so important to a man who couldn't even make a decent stab at shuffling the deck properly.

'All done Mrs Henderson, they feel just right now, should I turn them over?'

Rowena put out a hand to stop him, 'No John, I need to lay them out in a special way called the Celtic Cross first, then if you still want you can turn them over one at a time. That may seem unusual in card reading circles; however, I can't see that, who does what, will change the outcome.'

**

The reading progressed apace; each new card only had the simplest of messages for Rowena to share with John. She had explained that she would be honest about what she saw in the cards but that often the best interpretation would be in John's own heart and mind.

After a while she asked, 'So John, is it making sense to you so far? We have touched on an early love or emotion that relates to an older fair haired woman. That love was intuitive, the card of the Moon, the mother, but was held back or obstructed by a new emotional beginning, a new love. As far as learning goes you are doing well, nearly there, and your learning is strongly positive in direction,' she nodded to him to turn the next card.

For some reason John struggled to turn over this next card, almost as though he didn't want to know any more or it didn't want to know him, but slowly, the eight of spades came into view and he pressed it down firmly on the table.

John sensed Rowena's silence. 'Is this a bad card Mrs Henderson?' Rowena's mind was racing. 'No, not exactly bad John. . . I mean it could be or it might not be.' As Rowena looked across the table into John's face she could see the spectres of doubt and fear beginning to take hold of him. 'Okay John, it's not necessarily bad, it is the card of fate, it's the card of Saturn, and it also foretells of struggle or conflict. I can see these very things so clearly in you now, so this card and what it means, is most important for you.'

Rowena wasn't normally inclined to try and guide a client's thinking but she was going to make an exception in John's case. 'Right John, if indeed that is your real name, fate is not always bad, we just tend to think it is, but some might say the winner of the lottery was fated to win for some reason or another. It might have been fate that led you to the post office and to my little advert. . . was it fate that persuaded the nice people in the post office to give you my address? See, fate is not always the demon we make it out to be. Also consider the word struggle. Notice, John, in your cards there is no portent about losing; it merely tells us that you face a struggle. Whether you win or not is going to be up to you, the cards cannot give you any power, only an alternative prospect of self resolution. You can use that knowledge to make decisive choices knowing that though fate may intervene, destiny is always of your own making.'

'You are right, Mrs Henderson, I've been a fool most of my life, convinced that it was what others thought that should guide my life, I realise now that come what may, live or die, it must be by my own hand. I see it now, that my destiny belongs to me. My choices should be mine to create the most from the opportunities I have been given and so often refused or ignored in the past. Please continue Mrs Henderson, is there more the cards can tell?'

'There are four more cards to turn John, I'll go and put the kettle on again while you consider if you really want to know what else they have to say. . .' Rowena smiled, stood and wandered happily into the kitchen, time for another well earned cuppah and perhaps a biscuit too.

**

'Until you said what you said Mrs Henderson,' began John, 'it would never have occurred to me that there was ever a choice here. I've thought about it, deeply too, in such a short while, I don't need to see these other cards, I can probably predict what they will say. I'll enjoy that cup of tea and a biscuit with you, pay you for your time and be on my way. I thank you sincerely for your help. I already sense that at last I will be free.'

'You are most welcome John, you and the cards of fate have shared a journey of discovery together. They have shown you a direction and now you are on your own again. . . but I suspect, no longer lost.'

The china cups chinked once more in their saucers and the room felt good.

**

Two weeks later, Rowena was at work in the care home, tidying the empty day room, when she noticed a local newspaper opened on a page that straight way caught her eye. She knew that man in the photograph. It was John! She had been right, it wasn't his real name; he was in fact, Robert Hughs-Creighton the long lost son of Sir David Hughs-Creighton, Earl of Oakscombe.

Rowena picked up the newspaper and with only one thought on her mind sank deep into one of the comfy chairs. She began to read. . .

JOY RETURNS TO THE MANOR
Son and heir returns from the dead

Robert Hughs-Creighton, long lost son of Earl David Hughs-Creighton and who disappeared some ten years ago when aged 22, has last Tuesday night returned home to the joyful arms of his father.

A close family friend told our reporter, 'We all thought he was dead but here he is fit and well and large as life. When Robert's mother committed suicide after a long mental illness he was away at university. We never saw him again and not a word did we hear from anyone, despite extensive efforts by the Earl. Without any contact, David feared the worst and the Manor has been a very sad place for many years now. Tuesday evening late, the Earl answered a resolute knock on his door and there stood Robert, it was such a happy reunion, I can't tell you how much it means to friends and family to have the dear boy back home.'

The Echo's own Janie Simson managed to have a few words with the prodigal son himself and he had this to say.

'I'd like to say sorry to all those to whom I may have caused concern, it was never my intention. I merely followed my heart and while learning much about life at university it beckoned me to a new world and a new love. Nothing from then went well for me, life became one tortuous struggle, and conflict hunted me down daily. I began to fear I would follow in my good mother's footsteps and returned to this, my home town, to make my final peace with the world. In my moment of indecision, fate showed me a fortune teller's advert. It was as if it called to me like my mother called to me when I was young. I followed and listened. I shall be ever grateful for the wisdom and guidance I was given. So begins my life anew, this time I shall waste nothing. I thank you all for your time and understanding.'

Rowena let the newspaper fall to her lap and lent back in the chair. 'Should I too go home?' she wondered. 'Tonight I'll light that candle and read the cards just for me,' she smiled, 'and then we'll see, won't we?'

CHRISTMAS DINNER – THE INVITATION

It seemed impolite, not to accept the old couple's invitation to join them for Christmas dinner. Many years of living alone had made him resigned to doing his usual thing; for a change he thought he'd take up their kindly offer, despite only having met them at the bus stop the day before.

He arrived as requested, just before mid day. The old man, Bert, opened the door to him and with a squint into the brightness of normal daylight, grudgingly accepted the chocolates and wine and stood to one side. He was met by a strange mixture of odours, the overriding one emanating from the kitchen with a distinct burnt smell.

'Come on through,' said Bert, 'keep the warmth in. We don't open our windows till May, last year it wasn't till June. No, keep yer shoes on . . . or her damn dog'll 'ave em else.'

As his eyes slowly accustomed to the semi gloom he was glad he'd kept them on, the living room floor was littered with things the dog had discovered in months and years gone by. Bert used a stained, slippered foot to slide a full cat litter tray under a coffee table. 'Sit yerself down, make yerself comfortable, I'll go and tell herself you've arrived.'

He carefully chose the only chair that wasn't cluttered and sat down; he noted the décor, the like of which he'd not seen since his great uncle had passed away. As he heard a toilet flush somewhere in the house, a large long haired and unkempt brown dog rushed into the room and shoved its wet nose straight into his groin. As he struggled to push the excited animal away, herself came into the room holding out a wet hand to shake his.

'Bert,' she scolded, 'you should have told him not to sit there.' As he stood from the chair, his backside felt a little damp. Herself continued, 'his damn cat wet itself there yesterday.' She brushed her hand over the now warm dampness, 'not to worry, nearly dry now. Come on through, sit at the table.'

'Bert! For God's sake, don't let the dog do that, it's disgusting at dinner time.'

He was beginning to regret coming, life was better at home, still, perhaps the dinner would be good, I mean they couldn't have reached that age on bad food. 'You're worrying over nothing,' he told himself as he squeezed by the dog that had now transferred it's attention to twenty quid's worth of M&S chocolates which it eagerly bolted down, complete with wrappers.

What a relief, he needn't have worried; the table was set with bright clean cutlery and crockery. 'I bet they have a dish washer out back,' he thought, thinking further that it was an appliance he had long admired though never bought.

'You sit yourself at the head of the table dear. . . Bert! Throw that damn cat out into the garden.' Herself's tone softened and continued, 'I've already had to change the menu once today, the blessed thing mauled and gummed about the chicken breast I'd taken out of the freezer, try as I might, just couldn't save it I'm afraid . . . we've got sausages now. I take it you like sausages?'

Well this was going to be one novel Christmas dinner, one he'd never dreamed of and nor likely would anyone else. 'Yes, sausages will be fine, are they beef or pork?' he enquired, in as matter of fact tone as he could muster.

'Neither I think,' herself replied, brushing something indescribable off of her apron, 'we got a job lot off a traveller last year, he said they were venison. Could be or could be rabbit or perhaps even cat . . .' she laughed. 'Pity they didn't take Bert's old Fluffy at the same time.'

Candles lit in the table centre added a festive feel to the place, as well as a little warmth and were a welcome insurance against darkness should the electric meter run out.

Christmas Dinner - The Invitation

It was quite a posh set up with the food in large bowls from which you served yourself. 'Don't be shy, get stuck in,' she said, slapping Bert's hand. 'Let the gentleman go first, you wait your turn.'

Carefully, trying to take from the middles, he selected small portions of what transpired to be margarine and turnip mash, last year's de-frozen Brussels sprouts, a dark green cabbage with the most unchewable leaves he'd ever encountered and some small roasted potatoes, which actually seemed the best bet there, so he took extras. Bert smiled with pride as he watched his guest load up on roast potatoes, he'd dug them himself. Free they were, growing wild down by the sewage outfall. Must have been dumped at some time then self propagated from then on. Easy to dig too.

Herself lifted the lid on an old enamelled casserole dish to expose several burnt sausages. 'They're nice and well cooked, you can never be too careful with sausages I say,' she put three on his plate, three for Bert and two for herself, saving one for the dog later. 'I told Bert to put them in the fridge but thick that he is, he left them out in a warm kitchen overnight. . . I knew I should have done it myself.' She concluded her verbal assassination with a sigh.

As he ate the bits he'd chosen for his plate, the ones that looked most edible, and hacked the burnt crust off the curious tasting sausages, he felt his right foot becoming wet. His first thought was the cat had somehow sneaked back in but looking down, saw that it was the half retching dog, an excess of anticipatory drool flowing steadily from open, chocolate covered jaws to his socks and best suede shoes.

As he thought deeply about the foolishness of accepting this invite, he was shaken out of his mindful solitude by herself saying loudly, 'Eat up, there's plenty more, and I've made my own Christmas pudding, Bert even found some loose change in his pocket to put in there, so if you are lucky you could be going home with more than you came with.'

He felt his tummy rumble and watched as a large flea performed a double somersault on the way from dog to damp sock. 'Yes,' he thought, 'I'm sure you are right there.'

He looked at his watch and with pretence shock, yelled, 'Oh dear, I'm so sorry, is that the time, I just remembered I have to be home for a very important phone call. I'm sorry to dash off; it was really nice, thank you.'

'Would you like me to make up a doggy bag for your tea?' Herself asked kindly. When he graciously declined, she scraped the remaining bits of sausage onto Bert's plate and then placed it on the floor in front of an apparently ravenous brown dog, which in turn was probably feeding a couple of well established tape worms. As he stood in the doorway he watched in stunned silence as herself picked up the spotlessly clean plate from the floor and placed it back on the table. 'There,' she said, 'clean as a whistle and did you know, a dog's saliva is antibacterial. Almost better than a dishwasher Bert says . . and a lot cheaper.'

As he waved his goodbyes to an already closing door he wondered if the doctor's surgery might be running an emergency service, now all he had to do was make it back home and find out.

Happy Christmas.
By the way, what are you doing for dinner?

***

THE JOY OF CYCLING

Narwhal Bliss OBE was in his late fifties and had retired early on a banker's pension. Worn out by the pressures of a luxurious city life he had moved with his wife to rural Devon, a land of hills, trees and narrow lanes. He'd also taken up cycling. A state of the art racing bicycle and embarrassingly tight fitting and wasp like yellow and black racing lycra outfit had set him back about three and a half thousand pounds. Fortunately he couldn't be recognised when wearing his helmet, goggles and gossamer silk pollen-filtering scarf. This was the only reason his wife let him out. Lucinda found it an abhorrent almost disgusting sight and sought solace in gin and cream tea sessions at the country club with her friends. All had similar stories to tell.

It was 11.45 Friday morning and Narwhal Bliss was out for a ride, not too far, perhaps twelve miles or so. He chose the narrow coastal road for its fine woodlands, its twisting, bend filled treasures, high hedges and pretty flowers that leaned out across the tarmac. As he wobbled along slowly he felt the gentle breeze pass by, his helmet camera recording everything so he could play it back to his wife in the evening and his ears and mind filled with the sound of taped whale music. Bliss by name and Bliss was what he wanted. The road was his, not a soul in sight, except for an occasional vehicle travelling in the opposite direction. Some of them seemed to wave at him – he smiled and nodded back. How foolish people were, not to be out enjoying the countryside and this fine weather, still, it meant the road was his, all his.

Five yards behind the euphoric Narwhal, an old Devon farmer sat patiently in crawler gear listening to his catch-up box-set of The Archers, a few yards behind him was the full muck spreading bowser he was towing. At least a hundred vehicles had now joined the procession. Some would gladly have turned around and aborted their journey. This was not such a road. About half way back, a policeman had time to leave his car and book a woman for using her mobile phone. The fact that she was a midwife trying to organise alternative assistance for an imminent home birth, cut no ice with the policeman, whose bladder was likely to rupture if he didn't get relief soon. Two cars behind them and Bob Lovalot realised he would never get his girlfriend home before her husband was back from morning rugby training and he was already in trouble with his own wife for not remembering something she thought he should – whatever it was.

Life looked like a change was in the wind. And in the wind, was the rich farmyard aroma from the muck spreader aided by the fact it had sprung a leak. Two children on their way to school after a doctor's appointment threw up out of the back windows of a brand new Audi, their mother's screams clearly audible above the hooting of horns, threats and engine revvings.

'Oooooeeeeoooowww, oooieeow,' howled Narwhal as he sang along with the whale tape. He thought about stopping in a small and very rare lay-by but changed his mind at the last minute; after all, what was the point on such a fine day. He pedalled a little harder to see if he could catch up with a squirrel that was sitting on the road up ahead, peacefully scratching an ear with its foot. Narwhal glanced down at the electronic device on the handlebars, he didn't understand any of it, except the speed and that was in some foreign thing, not miles per hour, ah, eight, excellent, he was doing eight somethings. This pleased him, eight was nice number. He turned up the volume of his whale music, smiled and thought deeply about the number eight. How beautiful it was, its sound, its shape, its mathematical importance, chess boards have them, two to the power of three was eight. Though he wasn't completely sure about that, banking wasn't about maths as far as he remembered. Still eight was a lovely number.

The Joy of Cycling

Far behind him was a different sort of eight, in fact it sounded similar but began with an 'H'. Nobody could overtake safely, too risky with the tractor and trailer taking up so much room, even a deranged youth on fizzy drinks and driving his dad's Subaru decided it was a move too far.

Somewhere in a nearby town a judge was signing the arrest warrant for a young man stuck in car 74 and who had set off early so as not to miss his court appearance. An irate home owner was phoning around for another plumber and no, he didn't care what it cost, as long as the blighter turned up on time. Someone's dog had been in the house too long and, desperate to get out, it had urinated profusely on the best carpet and taken out its frustrations on the antique chair legs, splinters costing about fifty quid a time mixed with a rabid saliva as the pet took its revenge. The dog's oblivious owner turned to her friend in car 53 and said, 'Oh dear, little Flufkins will be waiting for me, probably sitting by the door waiting patiently for his mummy to come home.' Her friend, who was a cat lover anyway, simply drawled a long expressionless 'yeees', and stared out of the window at the unmoving scenery.

Narwhal's mind began to roam to food. He'd recently read about a muscle building bean curd and marmite sandwich in his cycling magazine, 'Cycling Supremos, magazine for the gifted elite', time to cycle back and try it out. With only half an unsighted glance behind him, Narwhal briefly flicked out his right arm, grabbed the bars again and slowly wobbled around to face his journey home.

His goggles were slightly steamed and in any event his spectacles couldn't be worn at the same time, so they weren't. He could see well enough for his own needs and was now amazed at the number of vehicles out on the road since he'd started out, how glad he was that he was turning for home. He certainly wouldn't want to get caught up in that traffic. The stench of overheating cars, diesel, petrol and some awful smell he'd never experienced in the City affronted his nostrils. Thank God he'd got a bike. As he passed by the now mostly stationary collection of motor vehicles he smiled and nodded back at those who seemed to be waving at him. 'Ah,' he thought, blessed are the cyclists, for they shall inherit the roads. See how loved we are.'

Narwhal waved, smiled and wobbled his way home, passing motorists exchanging accident details, motorists calling the AA for help, motorists in open war with their neighbours, partners, wives, children and a happy looking policeman watching from the other side of a hedge.

Narwhal switched on his second favourite cycling tape, 'Zoo animals in slumber', and to the sound of a snoring Galapagos tortoise, he dreamed of his sandwich and blissfully pedalled home.

Where would he go tomorrow?

No cyclists, squirrels or any other living creature were harmed in the making of this story.

***

Sally Ferdinando

Sally Ferdinando was born and brought up in North Devon. Living as she does in such a beautiful county, she derives a lot of her writing from her natural surroundings and her life as a farmer's wife. Her writing is largely drawn from life's experiences rather than the imagination.

THE POOL

Geoff, Margaret and Biddy, their youngest daughter, walked carefully over the damp grass clutching their precious cargo to their chests. As they walked over the rough ground, the water in their container slopped and slurped and it was all they could do not to spill the contents out on to the grass. Finally they reached their goal, knelt down, checked that all was okay and quietly slipped the container into the water. They had just released fifty frogs into the pond.

As they stood there watching, a small brown mouse scurried between the tall green stalks of the yellow irises. It seemed quite unaware that it had an audience and continued on its unhurried search for food. The frogs sat in an untidy heap for the first few seconds and then, discovering their freedom, they slowly dispersed amongst the prolific weeds that grew around the edge of the old concrete pool. The couple visiting the old house recalled the freezing cold water of the open-air swimming pool in their home town in the 1950s. Over the years it had been left empty to get steadily more of an eyesore. The new owners had ditched the pool in favour of turning it into a wild life feature, creating a large pond now boasting a new variety of creatures.

Geoff and Margaret thought back to the days of their youth, of the freedom and exuberance of their young lives. In the fifties heated swimming pools were rare – in fact swimming pools were a luxury. They had met at the pool, had a long courtship and finally married in the sixties. Coming back had stirred memories of the past. It didn't seem that long ago really that they had spent whole days here with their young friends. You could almost hear the voices, the shrieking, splashing and shouting that was the natural banter amongst teenagers. They looked at each other, embraced briefly and walked slowly back to the house, each just taking a moment to check on the frogs. There were none to be seen – they had merged into their natural habitat without a trace.

***

THE MILK RUN

Maisy Ayre sat in the back of her old car on this beautiful misty September morning and faced up to her day ahead. She had been in the business of delivering milk or milking the family dairy herd for most of her adult life, and a pretty good life it had been. As soon as she was old enough her father taught her how to milk the house cows, one a Jersey and one a Guernsey. She had loved them both with a passion and was always the first up to bring them into the shed for morning milking. As she got older she was given the more arduous task of bringing in the Jersey milking herd, putting them through the parlour, washing them down and, in latter years, learning how to use the modern milking machines. Having done the milking there was the butter to make and the scalding of the cream for the delicacy of clotted cream. Then the whey was given to the pigs. They only kept two and they had the run of the orchard.

In the early days many local farmers and neighbours would call at the parlour with their containers which they dipped into the tank and helped themselves to whatever they needed. Nowadays, she mused, this would not be allowed. Pasteurisation put a stop to that.

Well she had better get on. She had the milk delivery to do for all the terraced houses on the edge of town. There was Mrs Nott who lived on her own and who had a pint every two days. There was her paper to deliver too. She did not get out much so it was a good way to check up that she was alright and coping.

Then there was the young married couple next door with their new baby. Chaos reigned but the young mum was so pleased to see her and loved passing the time of day.

At No 3 was a newly widowed gentleman in his seventies. This one took longer as she was always persuaded in for a cup of tea and a biscuit. And, of course, there was the family from Nottingham who had recently moved and who were still completely lost with the slower way of life down here in the country. There were six children ranging between two and fourteen, all like peas in a pod and crowding out a house that was far too small for them. No doubt they would get used to country life but she wasn't convinced.

The list went on and if she sat here daydreaming any longer the job would not get done. She climbed out of the car, gathered up the milk and set off to do her round. There was still the evening milking to do when she finally got home but she would not have it any other way. It was a simple life, hard work but a good one.

RACKENFORD LAKE

Rackenford Lake sits in a deep hollow on what used to be known as the Rackenford Manor Estate in Devon. About two to three acres in size, it was dug out by hand many years ago.

It is probably one of the most beautiful and romantic spots you could possibly wish for and I have such happy memories of it. In the early days of our marriage we were lucky enough to live on the farm and this spring I was given permission to return there with a friend. It was a warm, sunny day and a real treat to go down memory lane.

The lake itself is surrounded by beech woods, ash and coppiced hazel, stunning in the spring with their lime green canopy providing a naturally cool place to hide out in the heat of the day. Willow trees grow in abundance in and around the water. In summer when walking around the perimeter of the lake, you have to step carefully to avoid disturbing adders basking in the sunshine. The water twitches with brown trout and golden carp. The carp are taking over in numbers, freezing the trout out. There is nearly always a heron perched on the old decaying wooden structure that we used as a diving board, now rotten to the core but still standing.

Canada geese are nesting this year on the small island, moorhens and wild duck forage on the outskirts amongst the weed and yellow irises flank the edge. The bluebells are still out, a magical blue and the smell of wild garlic pervades the air. The rhododendrons which were planted many years ago, provide a purple bloom to the banks surrounding the water.

Later in the summer the banks will be alive with purple patches of heather and wild flowers, the air filled with the steady drone of bees and dragon flies flitting over the water.

When my children were small and we lived just half a mile away, we would walk down there every day. The water was dark and peaty and swimming around the edges you encountered hot, warm and cold patches depending on where the sun had been. It was here that my boys first learnt to swim.

In the 1970s there was a real drought, water was scarce and we were all advised by the government of the time to 'bath with a friend'. The lake came into its own that year and every evening the children would be taken down there for a wash instead of the usual bath time routine. Nothing was more refreshing than a quick dip in the cool of the evening.

Family picnics, birthday parties and skinny dipping were a regular occurrence. There was seldom anyone around but family except on one occasion. A friend and I had risked exposure and gone for a wonderful skinny dip in the quiet of the evening and at the end of a long scorching hot day. When we emerged we were rather rattled to see a very elderly fisherman collecting his gear and silently slipping away. We never did discover who he was.

In the 1980s, when the children were a little older, we had a young vet student from Cambridge University to stay. She came to help with the lambing and in the summer she returned on many occasions bringing with her a delightful young man who was also studying to be a vet. He was a very keen windsurfer and, on spying the lake, he decided to teach us all how to windsurf. It was enjoyable and my only attempt at water sports, but it was not a success due to the unpredictable gusts of wind coming around every corner. Sadly in our day we never had the luxury of a boat, criminal really when you think of the fun we could have had. We did occasionally fish for trout from the bank. The boys got easily distracted when their lines got caught up in the surrounding trees, bushes and undergrowth so the effort of setting up a line for a few hours of frustration was more than it was worth.

Coming back to the present, our day of freedom had come to an end, as all good things do, and we made our way home up the track to the car at the end of the road. Maybe another day we could visit again.

JOINT STORIES

DOLPHINS   261

    Angela Nurse
    Richard Small
    Diana Warmington

NEW START   264

    Richard Small
    Angela Nurse
    Elizabeth Fowler

THE HOUSE MOVE   273

    Anne Smith
    Elizabeth Fowler

DOLPHINS

The first time I saw a dolphin, I was amazed at its size. We had arrived at the facilities for Dolphin Human Therapy in the Florida Keys where my niece was to receive support and therapy over the following few weeks. The dolphins were in a large lagoon where they spent their downtime, but they seemed to respond well to the arrival of humans.

Over the next few weeks we attended DHT every weekday morning and began to recognise the dolphins and their individual characteristics. During working hours some of the dolphins would work in smaller pools and provide the rewards or interact with the young children, all with profound disabilities. In many cases the impact of the therapy was remarkable. The chance of improvement in my niece's well-being was a possibility.

It was the first time I had been able to visit my niece since our trip to Florida. Her mother had already left for work, so we two had breakfast together. I asked if she still remembered the dolphins. She looked a little sheepish at first, then smiled and said, 'If I tell you, you must keep it a secret. . . promise?'

Put under such a spell and only ever wanting good for my niece, I agreed never to tell. It's a promise I am now about to break, I wonder if she will understand, for in the beginning, I don't think I did, but since those days, I also have dreams.

'Okay, auntie, you remember the dolphins, too, don't you?' I nodded as she continued. 'Well, they don't just live in my memory; I see them most nights in dreams. You see, we didn't go to them, they came to us. They tell me things that I can understand but can't explain. They are the chosen ones on the Earth. . . It's not us, you know, human beings. . . we just think we are. Dolphins are more Godlike than we can ever be, though God isn't a word they use, they use another word, which I hear in my dreams, and know its meaning even if I cannot say it now. I know deep down that all they do is connected to a universal consciousness; they are truly one with the Earth, it's a feeling thing.'

I was mesmerised by her voice and touched by her words, as she was touched by the dolphins. I just listened, unable to speak.

'We use them for our purposes, we use them for food, for entertainment, we drown them in our fishing nets, poison them with our plastics, but they know all this without losing their spiritual sense of being. They hope one day that we will learn from them, and also know. But time is running out, each night in my dreams I see that old friends are missing, soon there will be none left to visit me in the midnight ocean. The inexplicable cannot be taught – only learned.'

She put her spoon back in the empty bowl, looked up and smiled. I returned the smile and felt the connection between our hearts. I said nothing about the great wisdom she had shared; I didn't even know she knew such words, so clever for one still so young. Reaching across the table and touching her hand, 'Well, perhaps there is still something we can do to change the world...'

Looking back on those days, I recall all Claire, my very young niece had said, and from then on, watching her as she grew stronger both in mind and body, I felt it had been a privilege to be on hand and be a witness to her bonding with the dolphins. We met occasionally, her mother, my sister and I, and Claire was always in the news. Her dreams had continued, and the report wasn't always pleasant to hear. Her concerns about the dreadful deaths of dolphins, due to man's carelessness or downright evil, hurt her and took her mind off her schoolwork, which worried her parents greatly.

At the beginning of the September term, when she was 13, a new teacher arrived at the school, her subject being biology and environmental studies. Claire came rushing home from school that day, bursting with joy, at last the word 'environment' had been introduced into the curriculum. 'This is what I have been searching for, Mum,' she cried. 'I put my name down for Miss Briggs' group straightaway!' Her mother was almost in tears at the news. Depression had kept Claire on a downward spiral during the summer holiday. She seemed to seek out all the worst news in the press about sea life being damaged by shipping, climate change, dumping of waste, oil spills, until her mother felt like banning every newspaper and TV bulletin. But Hope was now at hand.

Time passed, and Claire's depression gradually faded with Miss Briggs' help and lessons on the subject closest to her heart. She had to neglect languages and art, because the sciences were far more important, and Claire was determined to settle her future on becoming an ecologist with environmental studies as a priority. At 17, Claire was looking up the universities who would give her the best course, and she chose Keele, and read out excitedly the subjects she would be studying.

'Listen to this, Mum! It's all here; geography, pollution control, natural resource management, ethics, law, and the best one, 'Crucial relationships between humans and the environment.' Now I shall really be able to do something to change the world.'

Claire's letters and emails are full of the wonder of the course she is following. She tells me it will be like a hobby that can give her a lifetime of work, doing the thing she cares about most, that crucial relationship between humans and the environment. I love to read her letters, and at the end of every one is a simple drawing of a dolphin.

***

NEW START

There was a knock at his door. The care warden popped her head around the side and said, 'Don't forget you start your writing group today. One o'clock, make sure you take the number 19 Green Bus south to Instow. Ask the driver to drop you off by the bookshop. . . OK?'

'Yes, yes, I know what I'm doing. . . I'm not a child you know,' he replied. Then, before the warden left. . . 'could you just tie my laces before you go and I don't suppose you've seen my watch anywhere?'

'Come here then, you've still got your slippers on – and your watch is on your wrist, no, not that one, the other one.'

By midday he was clutching a pen and empty note book and sitting on the upper deck of a number 23 Red Bus going north . . . and somewhere new. After about two hours the bus stopped in a strange town, the engines shuddered to a halt and the driver shouted 'All off, Terminus, everybody off.'

As he stepped off the bus platform he was greeted by a woman's voice, 'Allo ducky, fancy a good time?'

Pleasantly surprised to be met by someone from the writing group, he told her, 'I was told to go to the bookies first and then some club.'

She took him by the arm and walked him into William Hill's, kissed him on the cheek and promised they would go clubbing later.

He made a note in his new book, this was a great beginning. As he walked into the shop he couldn't see any books but there were a number of people sitting or standing around the room watching television screens. This was just like home and was not quite what he had expected. Nobody paid him any attention. Again, just like home. He thought perhaps he should check to see if he was in the right place for the creative writing group, so he walked up to the counter, taking a £10 note from his wallet in order to pay for his membership. He addressed the young woman behind the counter.

'Writing group?' he enquired.

The woman tapped something into the computer.

'Writer's Block?' she asked.

'Yes, that's right' the man replied.

She continued tapping.

'Five to four, 3.45, Doncaster.' She reached for the tenner and handed the man a receipt. 'Take a seat, it'll be starting shortly.'

The man was puzzled, five to four, three forty five, which was it? He looked at his watch. It was only half past three, he was in plenty of time. And who was Don Caster? He walked over to a seat and decided to watch the television while he waited for the group to start. Goodness, the other people here liked sport. There was football on one screen, horse racing on another and golf on a third.

When it got to four o'clock, no one else had appeared to join the group and he was beginning to feel thirsty. He wondered if he would get a cup of tea included in his membership fee. He returned to the woman behind the counter and showed her his ticket. She took it without a word and tapped into her computer again.

'Ooh, lucky you,' she remarked, handing him £22.50

The man opened his new notebook and made some notes. This was a place where he could more than double his money. He felt inspired. This would give him plenty to write about. This had been a most exciting afternoon.

As he left the bookies, he remembered he still hadn't had a cup of tea. He saw the friendly lady he'd met earlier. Gosh, she must be chilly standing around outside in those skimpy clothes in this cold weather. Perhaps he'd ask her if she would like to join him for a cup of tea and a warm up.

After a slight mix-up when she had suggested he must be feeling frisky, which he misheard as, 'was he wanting some whisky,' he explained that what he really wanted was a nice cup of tea and was there a tea room near by.

Thinking this over she realised there was no way she could take him into the Cosy Corner Tea Room, probably get them both thrown out as she was too well known. So what was she to do? She offered to take him home to her flat, but he was insistent that he would like a tea room and he fancied a nice cake.

Then an idea came to her, they usually had tea on offer in the afternoon down in the Liberal Club and as she knew several of the men who were members she should be able to get them a drink there. So off they set with her guiding him down Fore Street. He kept stopping to look in shop windows and was really enjoying himself. Passing the Hospice Charity shop he saw a nice green coat in the window, only £3, and he had just been given £22.

He commented to his new companion that she must be a bit chilly, so how about him buying her that coat. She agreed that she would be warmer in a nice coat, thinking to herself this was not what she was usually given, so in they went. The coat was just right and they added a scarf to the outfit. She felt splendid and realised she would be much more confident taking him for tea now that she was so well dressed.

Things got even better when they reached the Liberal Club as it was holding a big fund raising afternoon, with a full afternoon tea on offer at £6 a head. In they went arm in arm, which drew some risky comments from a few of the men, but she stared them down with a haughty look. The two of them handed over £12 and found a nice table in the corner.

No sooner were they settled and he was eagerly awaiting his tea, what a treat this afternoon was turning out to be, than a young lass came over and asked if they would like tickets for the big draw. This was the very last opportunity to buy tickets as the draw was to be made at the end of the afternoon. Even more excitement, a draw, he did like raffles, so 5 tickets were bought at a pound each.

Then they had scones and sandwiches and scrumptious cakes, what a change from the dreary Care Home tea. He ate and ate while the local band played on the stage, enjoying it all like a small school boy and they laughed at everything. Eventually they finished and she was beginning to wonder 'what now' when the big draw was announced. The local mayor was to draw the first prize and he made a long speech about the good work being done with all the money raised, praised the stalwart ticket sellers and announced that they had raised £16,000. Which drew loud applause from all the spectators.

Then, to a fanfare from the band, the winning ticket was drawn, ticket number 98 from book 16. It was one of the tickets sold just that afternoon, the two at their little corner table jumped up, that was his ticket. Up to the stage she propelled him where they were presented with an envelope. That did seem rather disappointing to him till the mayor said, 'Congratulations here are your two tickets for the Scottish Islands Holiday Cruise and £100 spending money.'

Giddy with this amazing and unexpected news the two of them ambled out onto the street. Now, what are you going to do with your prize she asked him, and he replied that he would jolly well go on this cruise and how about her coming with him. And then he would write a novel.

***

The pink and white splodge on the plate beside his tea did not even look edible to him and he thought back longingly to the wonderful tea he had enjoyed at that club he and Maggie had gone to, the club where he'd won his cruise holiday. What a day that had been and then cruising round the Scottish Islands with Maggie, she was such good company and he happily remembered all those daft and fun things they got up to together. His memento, the programme for that glorious trip, was in pride of place in his room.

But those ten fantastic days eventually came to an end when he said goodbye to Maggie as they disembarked. She had kissed him fondly and then driven off in the Rolls Royce that was at the dock waiting for one of the other gentlemen passengers. Oh well! it had been amazing, but now he was back in the

Care Home and daily facing an unappetising tea. Surely there was more to life than this, he really must do something. Another bus ride perhaps, would that be the answer? But where would he go? Did that matter? He'd not known where he was going last time and that turned out to be great.

So next morning he escaped, made his way to the bus stop and boarded the first bus to come along. Only needing to wave a bus pass meant he did not have to say where he was going, as he really had no idea, just see what happens. After almost a couple hours of wandering through villages and down country lanes the bus drove slowly along by the sea in a little seaside town. This was what he would do today, so pressing the bell he got off at the next stop.

The air smelt great, the sun shone and a little stall by the beach was selling fresh coffee, what could be better. Getting himself a cup he wandered to the wall above the beach and sat watching the world go by as he slowly drank his coffee. Gradually he got warmer and warmer in the sunshine, so off came his jacket. Then he thought the sea looked so inviting perhaps he would go for a paddle, not done that in more years than he could remember.

Once on the beach he removed his shoes and socks and put them carefully on a rock with his jacket before setting off across the sand. Reaching the water he cautiously walked in a short way, it felt wonderful, maybe he should have brought a swimming costume with him, if he actually had still had one. The water gently lapped around his ankles and as he watched he saw a little blue sparkle in the water, a little bit of sea-smoothed glass, just like the bits he used to find on the Cornish beaches when he was a boy.

He bent down to pick it up as a large friendly dog bounded over to say hello, unfortunately this made him lose his balance and he sat down with a splash in the water as the dog's owner rushed up frantically calling to the dog. In her hurry to help Harry she slipped on some seaweed and ended up sitting beside him in the water. She was distraught and so apologetic, but by now Harry was laughing, neither of them were hurt and it really was so silly, with the dog dancing around them as they sat fully clothed in the sea.

Susan stood up and reached out a hand to help Harry. By now she just couldn't help joining in with his laughter. Dripping wet they made their way hurriedly up the beach, collected Harry's shoes and jacket and made their way to Susan's car, where she gave him a car rug, told him to remove his wet trousers and wrap the rug around himself. Then they would go back to her house where she would dry his clothes in her tumble dryer.

A lot of discreet wriggling and giggling ensued as Harry got out of his wet trousers one side of the car and Susan removed her wet jeans on the other. Then they climbed into the car with Harry in his rug skirt and Susan in a long, droopy jumper that was really the dog's blanket. Once back at her house Susan gave Harry a pair of her husband's pyjama trousers to wear while his own trousers went through the dryer.

She asked him if he would be able to stay and have some lunch to try and make up for Bella knocking him over. It would only be soup and sandwiches, but she would like him to stay if he had nowhere he needed to be urgently. Then while she was organising lunch her two kids arrived home from tennis club, somewhat taken aback to find an elderly man in their kitchen wearing pyjamas.

After rather bemused explanations they all sat down to eat and Harry soon had them, by turns, laughing and totally enthralled as he told them about his time visiting the little harbours dotted around the Hebrides. Of rounding the tip of Cape Wrath through the wild currents driving in from the Atlantic and out of the North Sea and of lying up in Scarpa Flow, the Orkney harbour that played such an important role during the war. Maybe it was all a little larger than life and somehow they gained the idea that he was a kind of salty seadog of a sailor. It was all innocent fun.

After lunch it transpired they were planning a trip to the cinema and he found himself included in their plans. So equipped once more with his own trousers he got back into the car and they headed for town. He had not been to the cinema for probably 15 years and this would be so much better than old films on TV. The film they watched was a rollicking spy adventure, full of chases, shoot-outs, mysterious meetings and incredible special effects. Harry was quite amazed at the advances in film making and thoroughly enjoyed the afternoon.

Blinking in the bright sunlight as they left the cinema Harry asked the family if he could take them for a nice tea somewhere. The kids wanted to go to a new American Diner that had opened, so braving the flashy chrome and mirrored walls Harry went in with them to the loud strains of Elvis playing on a Juke Box. This was actually quite fun, took him back to his Teddy Boy days. They even had cakes with AmericanFrosting.

After their tea Harry realised he should think about making his way back. Susan was very keen to drive him home, but 'No', he insisted he was going back on the bus by himself. His adventures should have nothing to do with his life at the Care Home he decided. So he climbed onto his bus to a chorus of 'Bye Grandad, it has been fun'. In his hand was a memento of the day, a piece of pretty blue sea glass.

***

THE HOUSE MOVE

There was no gate across the path which led to the front door of the cottage. But a high hedge planted around the boundary afforded privacy to the house and garden. I walked up to the front door, which was standing open as the removal men were already unloading boxes from the van into the house, eager to be on their way. A small porch broke up the plain red brick wall. Tangled tendrils of honeysuckle and jagged rose stalks invaded the entrance, they would have to be cut back.

Stepping into the hall, the central room of the three downstairs, which was empty now save for a couple of packing cases, I stood for a moment trying to remember what I had seen on my brief first visit. I remembered there was a door closing off the staircase leading to the bedrooms above as is commonly found in old cottages. The small hall was square, and had probably served as a dining room at some stage as a fireplace was set into the wall adjoining the sitting room, where there was a back to back fireplace.

To the left of the hall lay the kitchen. I carried in the kettle and a box of basic provisions so that I could make the removal men a cup of tea. The kettle was boiling away cheerily by the time I rescued some mugs from my car. Walking back into the kitchen, I was stopped by a strange sense of something caressing my senses. What was that smell? There, just for a moment then gone, the sweet scent of violets.

I had rented this cottage to find a quiet place away from the turmoil and stress of life as an overseas news reporter and the loss of my partner, Andy, in a diving accident. It had been very much a spur of the moment idea, seeing the advert in a paper at the airport while I waited for yet another fog-delayed flight. I phoned the number given and on my return a week later had driven down to see the cottage one evening. The owner showed me around and I agreed to take it for a six month period.

My early life was very happy as the loved daughter of a single mother, school had been fine and then a job on a local newspaper which led quickly into the national press. But then mum died when I was 23 and I threw myself into the hectic world of reporting to escape the loss. Finding Andy six years later had been quite wonderful and we spent three magic years together till that devastating accident destroyed everything I had. For a year I rushed manically around the world always running from grief, on the edge of a breakdown, till I saw the advert and knew I had to stop and give myself time to mourn.

So I really knew very little about the cottage, renting it had just seemed the right thing to do at this stage in my life. It stood near the end of a little haphazard row, snug between its two neighbours, but with a very private garden across the front. I hoped my neighbours would not intrude on me and that I would find a sanctuary in this little house.

Having led a very peripatetic life I had few possessions, most of which which were now sitting in boxes around me waiting to find a home. I had bought a really good bed, as peaceful sleep was what I needed most. That was now in the bedroom upstairs, and the bed left in the cottage by the owner had been moved into the middle room. This would be fine for a visitor should I ever feel inclined to invite someone.

After they drank their tea and carefully moved my lovely Queen Anne table to sit in the hall, the removal men, with a cheerful wave, were on their way and I was alone at the beginning of a new life. I propped open the wide front door allowing the afternoon spring sunshine to flood in where it danced off the beautifully polished surface of my table.

The sitting room to the right of the hall was furnished with a large but dull, old chesterfield sofa. Thinking my Tunisian desert blanket would transform that I lifted it out of the box where it sat on top of my bits of glass and china. Laying it over the sofa its lovely russet colour burst into life in the sunshine streaming in, a couple of jewel bright cushions and the room came to life. There was even a wide window seat in here and I took my drink to sit on it in the life giving warmth and light. For the first time in a year I began to relax.

That evening passed in a gentle exploration of my new home, finding space for things I had brought with me and learning my way about. I rearranged the kitchen so that the table stood under the window looking out into the overgrown garden. That would be an early priority to tidy up and recreate a nice space. The sink and cooker were against the far wall and a pretty Welsh dresser stood opposite the window. I cleared the rather tatty china off this and displayed my own precious pieces, some with memories of life as a child. A mirror, which I hung on the back wall, made a big difference reflecting light into the room and a cheerful tablecloth completed my first reworking.

Supper was a dish of lasagne reheated in the cooker, washed down with rather too big a glass of wine. Suddenly I was totally overcome with tiredness, so made my way up to bed where I fell into an exhausted sleep. Just two hours later I was awake again and all the misery and loss of the past year overwhelmed me as I lay in the dark. I felt so alone, drugged with the misery of everything, unable to crawl out of the bed, but with a mind churning in distress.

Lying there curled up in the tangled bedclothes I imagined I heard a voice, a sweet gentle voice singing a lullaby. Straining to hear it my mind let go of the distress and gradually I slipped into a restful sleep. Each time I stirred, restlessly, I imagined that voice, till I woke in lovely morning sun. Slipping out of bed I crossed to the window and there again caught the slight scent of violets. Maybe they were growing below in the garden.

The day that followed was a pleasant one, making the cottage my own, cleaning where necessary and in the afternoon I ventured out to make a start in the garden. There was the path from the front door to the lane with an overgrown lawn on one side, and the remains of a vegetable area on the other. Flower beds had been created along under the windows where several plants were just starting to come through again. There were bulbs dying back in the beds, but I could find no sign of any violets growing there.

After exploring the small space the first job was to cut back the rampant growth around the front door, so I set off for town to equip myself with some basic tools. By the time the door had been cleared of the excess growth and the honeysuckle and climbing rose somewhat tamed the evening was drawing in and I was pleasantly tired out. Sitting eating my supper by the kitchen window surveying the garden, I was starting to make plans for all I could do and looking forward to creating something welcoming and pretty for myself.

By the end of the evening faced with a long dark night, all my distress came flooding back. The new bed was wonderfully comfortable, but sleep would not come and I tossed and turned in the dark, becoming feverish and disorientated till a cool hand rested lightly and gently on my shoulder. It brought such a feeling of tender care that I relaxed and slept. I had never suffered from visions and would not truly have been able to describe what was occurring, just that at moments of extreme distress, help and comfort came in a silent blessing, and I realised always, with that slight scent of violets.

I discovered that the cottage to my right was a holiday let and empty for now. While the cottage on the left, according to the postman belonged to Mr and Mrs Elmleigh who were away on holiday. I would meet them when they returned, but for now everything was peaceful and no one bothered me.

At the top of the narrow stairs in my cottage were two bedrooms and a bathroom which had a large, comfortable old fashioned bath, the sort you could really wallow in, but with a miserable hand held shower. That would need improving. As well as the toilet and basin there was a large cupboard with the back half raised over the stairs holding the hot water tank. The rest was empty but rather dark, useful storage if I had something big to store. In the gloom it appeared that there could have been an old door at the back.

Over the following week I settled in and began exploring my immediate neighbourhood, finding where to shop for the organic food I wanted to use. This proved to be a farm shop only a few miles away. I walked the riverside path that I could reach across the fields opposite the cottages, and enjoyed the peace and beauty I believed would allow me to recover my sense of worth and hope of a future. The nights could still be so cruel but the strange supernatural comfort that came at the most difficult hours gradually helped my mind to rest.

A few days later the Elmleighs returned and next morning I was invited in for coffee. They proved to be a delightful couple, easy to talk to and just the sort of neighbours I would have chosen. Their cottage was like mine except that where my kitchen was they had a dining room and the kitchen was behind, part of a single storey at the back which also held their bathroom. I was surprised that they had this large area downstairs when my cottage had just the three rooms.

This they easily explained. Apparently an elderly lady had owned my cottage and when finances got too difficult she sold the front of the cottage, sealed the joining wall and she now lived downstairs in the small rooms behind my cottage. She was a true recluse, never saw anyone, lived in silence, just sometimes walking in the woodland behind the cottages. I was most intrigued at the thought of my unknown neighbour. When I asked how she got her food and other basic needs, Mrs Elmleigh explained that she bought her a weekly shop, always exactly the same, and left it by her back gate.

According to local people who knew her earlier in her life she was a gentle, loving soul, adored by the children of the village, but had gradually withdrawn. They believed she was the widow of a man killed in the first year of the war and had no children. So she would have known the unhappiness I was suffering, I thought.

If you do ever meet her, Mr Elmleigh told me, the first thing you will notice is her Devon Violet perfume. A cold shiver went down my spine. Had I been dreaming all these past nights, or was there really a caring visitor who came in answer to my distress?

Edward Gaskell
publishers
DEVON

Writers Around
The
Mulberry Tree